I WILL BE THE
I CAN BE

The book starts with some highlights of a life's journey complicated by ADHD, and ends with guidelines for overcoming.

It has been written to help the ADHD community, but it will hopefully be of interest to everyone

ISBN: 978-0-244-61720-2

Dr Marius Potgieter

Available from Amazon as paperback and kindle and from Lulu.com and other outlets

I Will Be the Best Me I Can Be encourages the reader not to be afraid to be the best he or she can be. It is not intended to promote selfish ambition, but to encourage everyone to use what they have to its full potential.

The first part of the book consists of highlights from the author's life as a child, a student, a doctor and paediatrician. It is not an autobiography, just a collection of stories that will help the reader to remember the second part.

See part one as a 'primer'.

The second part is more specifically for those with symptoms of ADHD, whether or not they have been diagnosed with the condition.

The book is dedicated to

Andrea Bilbow OBE

The founder of ADDISS
(The National **A**ttention **D**eficit **D**isorder **I**nformation
and **S**upport **S**ervice.)

My hope is that the life-experiences I have written about will become alive in the heart and mind of the reader. I have not written about how things should have been, but how they were.

Table of Contents

6 About the Author

Part One
7 Once upon a time

Part Two
69 Foreword
72 The Heart of the Matter
82 Knowing my limits
83 Planning and Organising
100 Overcoming Poor Concentration
104 Developing Memory Power
108 Driving with AD
112 Suicide
114 Motor Co ordination
115 Perception
117 Specific Learning Disorders
119 Developing and Keeping Momentum
129 Money Management
133 Healthy Relationships
142 Overcoming Feelings of Failure
148 A Final Word

150 Appendix One
157 Appendix Two
161 Appendix Three

163 Useful Resources
166 Copyright Law and Legal Disclaimer

About the Author

Dr Marius Potgieter is a retired paediatrician who initially wrote a book for teens and adults called, *I Have ADHD/ADD – So What?* Followed by *I Will Be the Best Me I Can Be*, a motivational book based on the adult section. It is now updated and is intended to help anyone who needs some guidance in managing his or her life, whether they have been diagnosed with ADHD or not.

Dr Potgieter's life has taken him from working at two mission hospitals to being a private paediatrician in Pretoria, South Africa and also an associate professor at the Medical University of Southern Africa, MEDUNSA. During 1982 and 1983 he and his family were involved with Youth with a Mission, Hawaii, and he eventually went to work at St Peter's Hospital in Chertsey, Surrey from where he retired in 2011.

Dr Potgieter currently lives in Dorset, England, and is now a full-time carer for his wife, who has supported him for more than 54 years. He has children, grandchildren and greatgrandchildren in the UK, USA and South Africa, and friends all over the world.

Part One

Once upon a time…

There was a young boy who played behind the garage of the family home. Here he hollowed out the earth to make a dam. When he looked at the dam he had made, he had a dream that he wanted to make something really important. Something created by following his imagination. He started to make an irrigation system by channelling water from his dam into different canals and irrigating a piece of land where he planted some small plants and where he sowed some seed. He made a wheel which was turned by the running water and smaller dams downstream. On the sides, he planted what were supposed to be trees, and made other water projects as well. He made roads and bridges for his toy cars to go on and he thought all the time that one day when he grew up, he wanted to do something special in his life.

But when all was done, the water from his dam did not run strong enough for his project. He made a plan to get the water to surge by throwing stones into his dam. This worked really well, but he got so caught up that he did not notice that every time he threw a big stone onto the dam the whitewashed wall of the garage got muddy splashes. When his dad saw this, the project came to an abrupt end! But he did not let go of his dream...

As I am sure you can guess, that boy was me. Why am I telling you this story, and some others? Partly just for fun, but mainly so that you can have me in mind, conscious or subconscious, when you learn about ADHD in Part Two, and know that my advice stems from a lifetime of experience.

My mum was actually past childbearing age when I was on the way, unexpectedly I think, and she was very ill at the end of the pregnancy. I don't know if I needed resuscitation after birth, but I might have been a bit blue. I think they expected me to be a girl and give me the second name of my grandmother, Maria. When I pitched up male they called me Marius. I was christened on the very same day that the Second World War started. I could never work out if that was significant!

When I grew up everybody told me what a difficult baby I had been - apparently my elder brothers walked up and down the corridor with me at night to try and get me to sleep. As a young boy I wasn't good with relationships and got into lots of fights. I was always being told off for touching things I shouldn't have. I think I felt rejected by this and became quite rebellious. I felt as though, even when I did something with the best intentions, there was always 'something wrong with my attitude'. I did quite well at school in the early years, but later as the work increased I found it harder to concentrate and took ages to finish tasks. Once I asked my teacher why I took longer than the others, and he told me, "I think you are not thinking ahead."

After I decided I wanted to study to be a doctor, I made up for this by getting up and starting to study early in the morning when the others were still asleep. Even so, when I lost interest in class or during meetings I usually dropped off to sleep, even at university. Sometimes as a doctor I would travel half way around the world to attend a congress, just to lose concentration and fall asleep, and this despite many cups of coffee, Red Bull, biting my fingers and chewing my tongue. It wasn't narcolepsy, just an inability to concentrate.

I must tell you about one of my most embarrassing experiences at a conference. I was one of only a few who had to leave early due to flight connections. Unfortunately, there were no seats left near the door at the start and I had to pass behind the speaker when I left. As I did not want to disturb the meeting I walked out as quietly as I could, though in full view. Reaching the door, I went through and quickly closed it behind me, only to discover that I was not in the foyer but in a storeroom! It was pitch dark and I knew my only option was to go back into the lecture theatre to the amusement of everyone.

This also reminds me how embarrassed one of my classmates was one day. Our professor in Surgery was a wonderful teacher and none of us ever dozed off during his lectures. In order to remember our names he associated them with the part of the country we came from. So, at the beginning of the year he would go from one student to another, asking our names and where we came from – for instance: Jack Roberts, coming from Pietersburg (as it was then called). This student I want to tell you about, was late for the lecture and when the professor was looking the other way he slipped in and sat down. Unfortunately, he was the next student in line to be asked a question and he had no idea what was going on. The professor turned to him and asked his name and then, "Where did you come from?" He thought he was caught out for arriving late and his answer gave us all a good laugh; "I just had to go into town quickly, professor."

There was always good interaction between this professor and the class. He would call one of us down to examine a patient in the clinical classroom and if we took a bit long to speak up he would say things like, "What do you feel?" and, "Are you waiting for a message?"

One thing I learned early in my career is that there is no excuse for tiredness in a doctor who continues working day and night. Once the mother of a patient I saw late one afternoon said, "Doctor, I am so sick and tired of sick children."
"What about me?" I replied. "I did not sleep last night and today I've seen sick children all day long."
She looked at me without any sign of sympathy and said, "That was your choice."

Just before I leave the topic, we had another professor in whose class the students were on edge all the time. He always wore a bow tie and believed we should be well dressed when coming to his lectures. If one of us didn't have a tie on, he would say, "You there without a tie, get up!" And then pointing to the door, "Get out!" It rarely happened twice. One day he pointed in my direction, "You there, get up!" I turned my head to look at the student behind me – maybe he was talking to him. "I am talking to you with the blue shirt!" I got up. "Name the bacteria present in normal urine." I was not into my clinical years yet, but I knew about bacteria from my basic studies, so I named a few. His words made me feel very proud as he looked at the class and said, "Did you all hear what he said?" But then, oh dear, "It is all wrong! There are no bacteria in normal urine!" He expected us to complete the tasks he gave us on time – no exceptions. If we said we didn't have time, he would ask, "Did you sleep last night?" and if we said yes he would say, "Then you had time!"

We definitely had the necessary respect for our teachers when I was a student, but at the end-of-the-year class parties, we invited all of them and everyone enjoyed it. Later at a university where I worked, students who failed got others to demonstrate against the lecturer who failed them, trying to get him sacked. This is an example of not taking responsibility for your own actions but blaming others.

Both starting and finishing tasks could be an ordeal for me. Then there was also my forgetfulness, not in my medical work but in remembering to go to meetings on time if not reminded and recalling the names of people. I taught myself ways around this, like associating the person with someone else I know whose name was the same or nearly so, and by writing the name down in my pocket diary ASAP. Nowadays I suppose a mobile phone would be a better option.

I remember once when I was still a student I borrowed my dad's car to go to church and then walked back home with friends and clean forgot about the car. I went to university the next day and during the morning received a message from the Dean's office to call my dad urgently. "Where's my car?" he asked, and then I remembered!

Another time I answered the telephone and a sad voice said, "It is Ina" and then "My dad passed away this morning."
"Uncle Paul?" I asked.
"Yes" she said, but she did not hear me properly. Both Paul, my dad's brother, and Bill, our previous neighbour, had daughters with the name Ina and it was Bill who had died. I was under the impression it was Paul, my dad's brother. So, I told my older brother and he broke the sad news to my dad and the rest of the family who were at our home. Everyone cried and talked about the wonderful man Paul had been. Then my father and my brother drove to Paul's house to sympathise. Arriving at the front gate, they saw Paul's son-in-law in the garden, but he didn't look sad at all, on the contrary, he invited them in with a big smile on his face! My dad said to my brother, "There must be one big mistake here." He had hardly said it when the front door opened and Paul himself came out.

Needless to say, I got everyone's attention! I can remember my sister-in-law, who was quite a bit older than me, saying: "Marius if you want to become a doctor you must listen better to what people say and make sure about the facts before you tell others."
"I know," I said, and I did take her advice to heart. Fortunately, my dad wasn't angry with me; he was the one person whom I felt understood that I was not doing these things on purpose as others implied at times. These false accusations, rejection and my inability to realise my potential, made me feel quite depressed at times, but I could cope with it. I never consulted anyone about it or resorted to taking anti-depressants, though of course there are

some people who need to be treated in this way. Though I diagnosed myself, I never had a definite diagnosis of ADHD until I went to see a psychiatrist at the age of sixty-three, and he started me on Concerta, which I took for a number of years with good results. I will talk more about that later.

My dad also had problems with attentiveness and remembering things. He told me that when he studied in America he did exercises in concentration – keeping his eyes on objects moving around and other techniques that helped him learn how to concentrate. He was a very bright man, a good swimmer and a very good chess player. My mother once said to me, "Your father is a very clever man, just a bit slow." When I forget things now I am not afraid of Alzheimer's disease, because I have been like that all my life and I am actually a bit better now than when I was younger.

I may be accused of being impulsive, but I have done many things in my life which others hesitated to do. It may have landed me in trouble at times, especially when I was younger, but it has made my life much more worthwhile and exciting. Once, for instance, I went to a conference and stayed in a posh Central London hotel. When I went for a walk later the evening, I saw an old lady digging for food in a bin and felt so sorry for her. "Don't go away," I said, "please wait just here." I went into the hotel reception and with my credit card, I paid in full for a luxury room with a shower for one night. I can't remember which name I used, but as I walked towards the front door I heard one of the staff saying to the other, "He is going to get his lady for the night." You should have seen their faces when I brought her in; wearing dirty clothes and carrying a supermarket bag with food from the bin! One man took it from her with just his thumb and the tip of his index finger, so as not to touch too much of it, and dropped it in a bin. They did show her to the room, as it was already paid for, including room service, and when they asked her what she wanted, she said, "Just a cup-a- tea and a sandwich please." She was still in the room the next morning and I did not see her again before I left.

I always wondered whether she had used the shower!

I will be telling you more of my life stories, which may or may not have to do with my ADHD, but all of them will incorporate my 'best me.' My purpose is not to boast about my accomplishments, far from it, but to encourage you to be the best you can be in your own particular life situation. And remember everyone's best is different. I would like to ask you very earnestly, please don't compare yourself with me, or for that matter with anybody else, only with your own personal best.

As a student, early during my clinical experience in medicine, I went to see what was happening on Saturday evenings in our local A&E. This was something not even senior medical students were interested in doing, but I found it fascinating and went there regularly. It was a time that many drunk people were brought in and knife wounds were the order of the day. As I was watching the doctors stitch up wounds and refer more serious cases to the theatre for emergency surgery, they came to know me and later taught me how to clean wounds and put in stitches. Later they left me very much on my own to treat minor wounds. Nevertheless, I learned a lot and frequently accompanied the patients with major injuries, like penetrating wounds to the chest and abdomen, to theatre. Sometimes there were neurosurgical emergencies, and I accompanied some of these to theatre.

After finishing my studies and doing my hospital year, I got married and my wife and I went to live and work on a mission station where there was a hospital. It was quite far away from other hospitals and the two other doctors and I had to treat most of the patients who came to us.

I was the junior (left) and the other two doctors, Dr Herman Visagie (centre) and Dr Willie Scholtz (right) helped and taught me a lot.

Sometimes, however, I was left on my own, because one of my colleagues might be away on holiday and the other witnessing in court, as we were District Surgeons as well. I could tell you many stories about my life and work there, but this is what happened one day when I was the only doctor in the hospital and I just had to be my best me…

She arrived by ambulance in a subconscious state, a young girl of about eight years old who had fallen from a tree and injured her head. When I examined her it was obvious that she had an intracranial bleed. Her consciousness further deteriorated after admission, she no longer responded to pain stimuli, one of her pupils was larger than the other and not reacting to light. I knew this was a neurosurgical emergency and I felt out of my depth, so I called a neurosurgeon who was more than two hundred miles away. He concluded that there was no way that she would survive a transfer. "Have you got a Trephine?" he asked.

A trephine is an instrument used to remove a disc of bone from the skull. We had one, which had never been used. I had seen one being used once or twice during the time I attended A&E, but I had never used one myself. The neurosurgeon said that was my only option. From the swelling on the side of her head where she had hit the ground when she fell, and from other clinical signs, I decided where to make an incision and bore a hole through her skull with the Trephine. I knew it was the right place when blood gushed out, clearly under pressure from what we had decided was an extradural haematoma (no scans available). Blood drained for some time but no cerebrospinal fluid. We were delighted to see her consciousness improve, and after two days she was sitting up in bed and later went home with just some weakness on the one side. The parents were very grateful and so was the doctor.

On another occasion, I just had to get help, however difficult it might be. Again I was the only doctor at the hospital when a woman was admitted in a shocked state. She was in labour, but it was not progressing because of her narrow pelvis. By the time she was brought in the baby had already died and there were signs that her uterus had ruptured. This called for an emergency laparotomy (opening of her abdomen) and probably a hysterectomy. I have done many hysterectomies, but not under these circumstances. I got hold of Dr Grant, who was a surgeon, at a hospital in an even more remote area than us. Though he was the only doctor at his hospital, he made the long journey to come and help me. I kept the patient going with blood transfusions and administered the anaesthetic for Dr Grant to operate. It was a very difficult operation, but the patient survived. I was so thankful that I had recognised my limitations.

We did many caesarean sections. I don't know I was fast or slow because I am not comparing myself with others, but I could do a complete caesarean section in thirty minutes. There is a saying that 'practice makes perfect'. I wasn't perfect but I got a lot of practice. One thing I learnt by doing the operation was that, if I really had to, I could concentrate. When doing a caesarean section, from the moment you make the incision in the uterus until you deliver the baby's head and body, you have very limited time, because during that period the baby's oxygen supply is interfered with. Anyway, when I made the incision and put my hand through to get the baby's head out, it felt to me as if the rest of the theatre got dark or even vanished. For that period nothing else mattered and I think I concentrated one hundred percent to get the head out ASAP.

It did not happen many times, but on a few occasions, I had to start the anaesthetic, ask a nurse to watch the patient closely, get ready to operate and, with the nurse assisting, do the caesarean section. If the baby had problems, the assistant just had hold a swab on the incision in the uterus and push down hard until I could come back and stitch up the wounds. Nowadays specialist nurses to do all kinds of things traditionally done by doctors, but back then they did not even take blood or put up an intravenous infusion. However, I could never have done without them.

We also did many cataract operations. My colleagues taught me how to do it. The patients who came to us were usually aged with snow-white lenses and no vision except for some light perception. After the operation, they kept the eye patch on for three days and then removed it; we then gave them standard corrective glasses. It was such a joy to watch them as they laughed and shouted and cried, all at the same time. Any sight was just wonderful to them, as they had been blind for many years.

A very serious condition that new-born babies may develop is Tetanus neonatorum. It is caused by the tetanus germ that enters the baby's system through the umbilical cord and before we had our educational and immunisation programs fully in place, we had a lot of these babies, due to the traditional belief that cow dung, which often contains the Tetanus bacterium, should be put on the cord after birth, either because of superstition or presumably to stop the cord from bleeding. The first sign was that the baby could no longer feed properly, as the jaw became stiff, and it would later start having seizures. A high percentage would die, even when we tried our best to save them. Anyhow it wasn't so easy to stop the practice as the traditional doctors advocated it and we first had to gain the people's trust, which came with time. Later we seldom if ever saw babies develop this terrible condition.

It was very hot there. We did not have air conditioning and went home for a siesta at 12 noon, returning at 3 o'clock until 6 during the summertime. There were mosquitos and malaria, so the hospital and our homes had mosquito mesh in front of all the windows and we sprayed them as soon as we saw a mosquito. The water pools near the hospital were sprayed with a very thin layer of oil to stop the mosquitos from hatching. Because of the heat we had an enclosed veranda or 'stoep' attached to our bedroom which was big enough for our bed. There was no lack of water and, because my wife was expecting our first child and so uncomfortable in the heat, I put the garden sprayer on top of the roof at night and the spray falling in front of it brought some coolness to the veranda where we slept, while watering the lawn as well.

One very painful lesson I learned because of not being my "best me" was this one. I got a lovely Alsatian puppy, which I named Cindy. I adored her, but I did not take the time to "train her in the way that she should go." She was very obedient in the sense that, if you told her to come or not to come, she would either come or not come! She started stealing things. We went on holiday and left her with one of the staff on the mission station and when we returned people were not as friendly with us as usual. We heard different stories about what our dog had done. The lady in charge of the nurses' home told us she had prepared the meat for the week, then she went to fetch something from her room and when she looked out of the window, there was Cindy running away with something quite big in her mouth. When she got back the kitchen door was open and the meat was gone! We only got supplies once a week which made it worse.

There were a lot of other complaints. One lady baked a birthday cake and Cindy was still gulping it down when she came into the kitchen. She knew exactly how to open a door. Even more worrying, she got aggressive when she was caught in the act.
Nobody else wanted to do it, so I had to put her down myself and as I sat down beside the lifeless body of my dog, I was as sad as anyone could be who destroyed his own dream. Maybe if there had been one of the dog trainers that we sometimes see on TV around we could have saved her, but there wasn't.

Another thing I learned was that the more you know about a certain subject, the more interesting it becomes. I saw many patients with tuberculosis and for me it wasn't really interesting to treat them, though we had good results in general. Then I went to work for a month in a hospital that was a centre of excellence in the treatment of chest conditions, including TB. When I learned about the best management of the condition and more signs of the disease to be on the lookout for, it changed my attitude towards the patients. It also taught me that one must never stop learning, therefore, as I will describe in the second part, I still keep some 'protected time' on a Thursday for studying or further reading. Even whilst retired I have to keep on learning, otherwise my brain goes 'limp.'

I performed post mortem examinations on every patient that died to see if there was more I could have done, so that I could do it better next time. There were not many of them; most post mortems we had to do were for medico-legal reasons. One patient I remember who died in A&E was a school teacher who had drunk too much beer. His choking reflexes were suppressed by the high level of alcohol and, when he regurgitated volumes of beer, he literally drowned in it before we could help him.

Once I was really put to the test. A man hanged himself – about a week before, as we later concluded – and was hanging there in the hut when I opened the door. The police stood at a distance with handkerchiefs over their noses, and I had to ascertain that he did not sustain injuries like stab wounds or a fractured skull from someone who could have hung him there. I had to spray the flies before I could do anything else. I won't go into further detail, but I did finish the job. On another occasion, they brought me to a hut which had been struck by lightning. I could not do much, as all five of the people inside were burned and unrecognisable, some like large pieces of charcoal.

I think I must have seen one of the last cases of smallpox; the patient was placed some way from the hospital in a tent. It was an awful thing to see and the eradication of this terrible disease is a great medical accomplishment.

At the mission station, the guys for some reason always looked at my hair to decide when to have a haircut evening. It was a joke, for I have not got much hair, and reminded me of how I started to lose my hair when I was still a student. My mother felt so sorry for me that she gave me money to see someone who advertised in the local newspaper that he did an assessment and then gave you the right medicine to make your hair grow. He had a posh office in the city centre with several pictures on the walls of men's heads bald before, and their hair growth after treatment; this really made me excited. After taking my money, he took me to a side room, told me to sit down, and then looked at my head with a magnifying glass. "Hmmm, hmmm" he said over and over and then, still looking at my head asked: "How many times do you wash your hair per week?" I told him once or twice, and he went on for another few times, "Hmmm, hmmm," and that was it! I did not feel guilty at all, because I kept myself clean and well-groomed after a girl I really cared for at school dumped me, allegedly because of dirty fingernails. I don't know if that was the only reason, but that was what she said in a little letter she sent me inside a blue envelope. The man poured a yellowish liquid into a bottle, wrote my name and the directions on the label, and said good bye. As I left with the bottle of stuff to massage into my scalp, he called in another sucker!

Back to the hair-cut evening, which was really a men's social, and it was one of the doctors who cut the hair. He related to us that when he went to boarding school, his dad gave him a set of hair clippers, scissors and a comb and said that was his pocket money for the next five years. He taught himself to do haircuts – the first ones may not have been very successful - but he became so good at it that he always had more pocket money than most of the other kids.

I was asked to help start another hospital, which was newly built by the government. They offered me the position of Superintendent and I accepted it which, looking back, I don't think was a wise decision, as there was too much admin work involved and I was the only doctor. I still remember the difficult times I had, sitting in my office working through the stacks of paperwork, trying to motivate myself to do it and feeling as though I was being lazy. Though I knew that it was more than just laziness, I was motivated by something one of our professors always said: "The only remedy for laziness is work!" I would jump up from my chair, walk to the window and take a deep breath, go back to my chair, maybe slap my hand on the table, and then sit down to apply myself to the workload. This had some limited success. Later I found that splitting the pile of paperwork into several smaller piles helped to motivate me as I saw them disappear one by one. I also delegated much of the paperwork to the secretary, but there was still lots that needed my attention. What also motivated me was that the salary was good and it was the only time in my life that a bank manager called me to ask why I was not making use of the available overdraft on my account!

One important thing I learned was to finish one job before you start another. If a job is worth doing, do it and finish it, even if there are many others pressing for your time. If you have to go back to finish, it takes longer to complete and you are dragging the weight of unfinished work behind you all the time. I got this right and started to finish task by task, giving my attention to one problem at a time. I also learned to be flexible when an emergency or a high-priority problem came up, becoming steadfast, but not rigid. As time went by I internalised these guidelines and, when a situation arose, I could 'shoot from the hip' or think on my feet, without pondering over every eventuality before I could respond. I had learned a lot from my colleagues at the previous hospital and I definitely had to use it…

The new hospital building was completed and all the furniture was in place. The theatre was well equipped and there was even air conditioning, but there were no patients yet! The builders were clearing the premises when one of them came running into the hospital shouting that a worker had fallen under a lorry and one of the wheels had run over what sounded like his abdomen. On examination, he was clearly having serious internal bleeding. We took him to the theatre and the Matron quickly sterilised the instruments. Fortunately, there was another hospital not so far away and a doctor was available to give the anaesthetic with a nurse assisting me. When I opened the abdomen, it was one pool of blood. The liver was split in two and right in the middle there was a severed artery pumping blood. I tied this artery and with a large semi-circular needle I put several stitches through both parts of the liver to hold it together. The doctor who gave the anaesthetic sucked up the blood from inside the abdomen with vacuum bottles through a filter and transfused the patient with it. It was remarkable that apart from a few rib fractures and soft-tissue injuries the patient did not sustain anything more serious and walked out of the hospital ten days later.

I learned not to strive to always be the best, but strive to give my best. After working in the mission hospital for several years, I went back to university and specialised in paediatrics. I will tell you about that later, but for now, let's return to a few things that happened during my school years.

Just after I entered school, the teacher gave each one of the class a reading book. Some were old and some were new; mine had a cover but the book had been used a lot over the years. I looked around and there was one girl with a brand-new uncovered book! During play time, I took my book from the cover, placed it on the girl's table and slipped her book into my cover. (Makes you think about the story of Cindy, doesn't it?) After the break, there was trouble! The girl told the teacher and she made us all line up.

"Marius, you can sit down, yours has a cover." Later after she looked at all the books and did not find the new one she had given to the girl; her eyes came to rest on me. "Maybe you should bring me your book also!" The next thing was that I found myself in the head-teacher's office. He happened to be my dad. The teacher explained the situation and left.

"Did you do it?" my dad asked.

I denied it; "Someone else must have slipped the book into my cover." My dad did not buy my story and I got a hiding. (Only the head teacher was allowed to give hidings) At home my dad did not talk about it, but the next day I was summand to the office, still denied it and got another hiding. This happened on three consecutive days, the last time on the Friday. Even then I kept on saying I didn't do it.

Then my dad said: "No more hidings for you; come and tell me if you did it." I put my arms around his neck and started to sob, "Yes, Dad, I did it!"

There had always been a good relationship between me and my dad, even after he had disciplined me. He never disciplined us in anger and always gave us a chance to explain first. I was thinking later, three consecutive hidings were a lot, but if he had just given me a warning on the first day, would I not perhaps have stolen things again? I learned later that the best way to stop a child taking things, for instance from a shop, is to send him back with the item (if he hasn't eaten it!) to apologise and pay for it with his pocket money. It may be wise for the parent to accompany the child.

If it is done without anger and under control, some boys will respond better to a good hiding than to many words of reprimand. I know of youngsters who boast about how many times they spent a night at the police station after they had done wrong, where they got coffee to drink and TV to watch. I think if the officer in charge was allowed to give them a few good stripes, they would be less inclined to go there next time!

My mum was a lovely straightforward person. Once, I remember, two of the children in our primary school allegedly had sex. All the boys, including me, talked about it, discussing in detail how it could have happened. I had to fetch something from home when my Mum cornered me. "Did you hear the nasty stories about so and so?"
"Yes" I said.
"I hear you were one of the boys talking about it?"
"Never!" I said. She seemed to believe me.
"Now I tell you what you do; when you go back to school, go and put these lies about you straight!"
"Yes Mum," and off I went.
I knew she was going to ask me if I'd done it, so I said to some of the boys, "You know those stories about..." I mentioned their names, I wasn't quite sure what I was going to say, as long as I could tell my mum I spoke to them. "Don't start talking about that again, you will get us all into trouble!" That was the end of my effort to 'put things straight'!

My mum died of cancer when I was in my final year at medical school and that was a real setback for me. I became unwell and was lying in bed when the lady who worked in the office attached to our home came to me and said, "Marius, I just want to tell you this, God went into his garden and picked for himself the most beautiful rose." The words may sound like just rhetoric, but at that moment of sadness in my life, they were the most beautiful I have ever heard. I knew my mum always wanted the best for me, so I went back and finished my studies. She actually toiled the last years of her life to help me through university. I was taking this for granted until suddenly one day, without anyone talking about it to me, it struck me how much she was doing for me. I considered how much effort, for instance, went into preparing a meal to be ready for me when I came home. From that day on I made a point of thanking her whenever she did something for me.

Parents can be strict on their children, as long as they spend time with them and do things together. One of our lecturers was very strict with his lovely daughters – just as an example, a boy carrying their suitcases from the car, had to leave them in the front room; he was not allowed to take them to the daughters' rooms. One of his daughters was in our class at medical school and she told us that she had a friend whose parents allowed her to do whatever she wanted. This friend said to her one day, "I wish my parents loved me as much as your parents love you, not allowing you to do all the things my parents allow me to do." Of course, overprotection may also make children feel unloved and not secure in acting for themselves.

Before I leave my childhood behind, there are a few more experiences I want to tell you about. When I six I walked around with this piece of iron in my mouth. Suddenly it slipped down my throat and I inhaled it. I still remember the terrible coughing episodes I developed, but I told nobody about the piece of metal. My mum gave me all kinds of cough mixtures and they later took me to the doctor. I don't know what his diagnosis was but his medicine didn't help me. That evening in bed I had a terrible coughing spell and I coughed it out and swallowed it, but it was now in my tummy and not in my airways. The cough subsided immediately. I think my parents thought the doctor's medicine had worked.

Our neighbours had a dam on their smallholding and we children always went to swim there. One day when we arrived the woman of the place was walking with two women supporting her, one on each side. She was crying loudly and the words we could make out were: "Doctor has killed my husband, doctor has killed my husband…!" The doctor's car was still there. He had probably tried unsuccessfully to save the man's life by giving him an injection or something, but the woman did not interpret it like that, and neither did we when we heard what she was saying. We grabbed our things and ran for dear life, with a picture in our mind of a killer doctor running after us with a great big syringe!

At this stage, I must really tell you about one last childhood incident that happened on our farm, in what is now called, Botswana. This was wild country, but I was never confronted by a lion as I walked around all over the place with my .22 gun. One day, however, I had a scary experience when I was with a friend of mine who visited with us. We were riding along on a donkey cart when the donkeys must have smelled a lion and they started running as fast as they could, first along the path and then through the bushes and over ant hills.

We saw the trees on all sides of us and we were both afraid that the two donkeys would pass one either side of a tree and that the cart would then smash into it, so my friend decided to jump! He was quite a heavy chap and as I looked back I saw him strike a young Mopan tree which was bent over by his weight. He had a reasonably soft landing on the grass, as the tree swept him back, but at that very moment it occurred to him that the donkeys might be bolting from a lion, so he got up and ran so fast that he actually passed the cart, and managed to stop the donkeys. We were scared but got home safe.

After finishing my six years as medical student I did my hospital year as house doctor (intern) starting in the Department of Obstetrics and Gynaecology. During the time that I worked there I had one of the most traumatic experiences of my medical career, when I was, of course, still young and vulnerable.

A woman was referred to the Department, whose babies died soon after birth due to Rhesus sensitisation, where the mother develops antibodies against her unborn baby's red blood cells. These antibodies, like other antibodies that protect the baby against certain infections, go through the placental membrane that divides the mother and baby's blood circulations, and destroy the baby's red blood cells. She needed specialised management to try and save the next baby. What was offered to the mother was that she would be admitted to the maternity hospital and we would monitor the baby's intrauterine development very closely to decide when it would no longer be safe for the baby to stay in its mother's womb due to the effect of the antibodies. At this stage, the baby would be delivered by caesarean section, and the paediatrician would do an exchange blood transfusion immediately. Monitoring the baby's condition clinically was delegated to me, for about ten days I did it diligently and the mother and I became quite well acquainted as I listened to the baby's heartbeat many times a day. At the point that the heart beat changed due to the baby becoming stressed, an emergency caesarean section was done early one evening, supposedly just at the right time – about thirty-four weeks' pregnancy. The baby was already slightly yellow, and pale but otherwise looked fine and even better after the exchange transfusion was done while he was still in theatre. More exchange transfusions were planned. From the theatre, he went to the neonatal unit, snugly wrapped up and placed in an incubator, supposedly only for the first few hours as he didn't seem to need it. When the mother awoke from the anaesthetic, they took him to her and she held him for a short while. She was so happy.

I was called to the neonatal unit later the evening by the nurse, as I was on the premises and it would have taken a paediatric doctor longer to get there. I saw that something was seriously wrong with the baby; the wrapping around him was soaked with blood, and he was very pale with irregular breathing. I acted as fast as I could, starting an IV infusion. Rh negative blood was available and I started giving it immediately and also gave adrenalin when his heart beat went down. The paediatric doctor came, we did all we could, but we lost him just after midnight because of irreversible shock due to severe blood loss from the umbilical vessel. The umbilical tie had slipped off, and due to him being covered, the bleeding was noticed too late. I blamed myself for not insisting that the baby lie uncovered in the incubator for better observation, but the real traumatic moment followed when I went to tell the mother. As I entered, I could see she was awake in the dim hospital light that was kept on in the room during the night.

"Doctor I am so happy, the baby is beautiful, isn't he?"

"He started to bleed a bit," I knew immediately how much of an understatement that was, but I was at odds as to how to start telling her the truth.

"But he is OK?"

"Not really" I said.

"You mean? You mean?"

"Yes, he lost too much blood from the vein through which the exchange transfusion was done and he died in spite of all we tried to do to keep him alive."

I will never forget the expression on her face and her cry which reached far beyond the hospital room that early morning. "Please, please doctor, tell me he is still alive!" At this point, I could no longer control my feelings, and when some of the other staff came I was crying unashamed there with her.

After I qualified as a paediatrician, I went to look at facilities for handicapped children in the UK and Holland, then Linda and I went on a tour through Europe.

Returning home, I started a private paediatric practice in Pretoria. This is one of the university cities of South Africa. October is summertime and the Jacaranda trees are in bloom.

I treated many patients daily in my rooms, in hospitals, attended caesarean sections and treated a number of babies in the maternity hospitals. I read an article about a method to treat new-born babies with respiratory distress and made an apparatus to apply continuous positive airway pressure (CPAP) to their lungs, with good results. Later when we could purchase the sophisticated apparatus to do it, I was already doing it.

Maybe because of my impulsivity and impatience I started to use neon lights on babies with jaundice while the other paediatricians still waited for more studies to be done before they started; later this became common practice. Before that we had done numerous exchange blood transfusions, so this also solved the problem of parents who were Jehovah's Witnesses and refused any blood transfusions, as it is against their belief. Though I respect their beliefs, I once had to resort to a court order to do an exchange transfusion on a baby who might have developed brain damage (Kernicterus) if I did nothing about the high bilirubin level. The same with Ritalin, I was the first to treat my patients with it and of course this also became common practice later.

In the examples I mentioned, all turned out well, but it is risky to use medicine that is not fully approved for a specific condition. A colleague was not so lucky; he used Diazepam (a sedative) for babies with severe colic. It worked so well for them that it boosted his practice, but then one day a baby died – probably of another reason – but because he received Diazepam it was implicated and the doctor was in real trouble for using a medicine not licensed for the condition.

I could tell you many stories about the patients I treated, but there is one I want to share with you for a reason. A GP from a nearby town phoned me to ask if he could refer a boy of about six years old for my opinion because this patient had developed a cough and now couldn't stop coughing. I specifically asked if he had inhaled something and the doctor said there was no history of it. The coughing did subside for periods and then got worse again. I was very busy in my rooms and decided to admit him straight to the children's ward and arrange for a chest x-ray. They would call me if there was anything serious on the x-ray picture, otherwise I would see him after surgery. He went for the x-ray, but before there was even time to develop the pictures, while he was still in the x-ray department, he started choking severely and stopped breathing. They couldn't do anything for him and called me to say my patient died. I left all the patients at my rooms waiting and went there. By the time I arrived, the x-ray was developed and just there in the middle of the trachea was a screw which he inhaled. It must have come to rest in this particular obstructive position when he got up after the X-ray was taken. I thought a lot about this patient, and also about the time I inhaled a piece of metal. Could I have done more to prevent this tragic loss of a young life? I don't know. Maybe I could have pressed the referring doctor more to make sure of the possibility that the child had inhaled a foreign body, but would the child have told them? I didn't.

Anyhow from that time on I was much more on my guard for a repeat of what happened, but it did not recur, even though I practised as a paediatrician for about another thirty years.

I did work very, very hard and paid a lot of income tax (73% at one stage) One of my colleagues wrote a letter to the receiver of revenue addressed as follows: "Dear receiver of all my income." Anyhow, I remember one night at about midnight I was so tired when I went home that I just stopped the car at the side of the road and got sick. My wife knew what she was in for by marrying a doctor and she managed the children mostly on her own, though two of our children had problems involving many hospital appointments.

Actually, our daughter, Linmari, was born prematurely by caesarean section, because she started to show signs of foetal distress No ventilators were available, so the paediatrician who attended her, ventilated her by hand all night. In the early hours of the morning, I decided to go home for a short while to get ready for the day – I was half way through my specialist training at that time. As soon as I reached home the telephone rang, it was the hospital and the nurse said I must come immediately because the baby's heart had stopped and the doctor had stopped ventilating her. It was clear to me that she could no longer be alive, but still as I drove to the hospital, I kept on praying that she would live. At the back of my mind was the memory of that other baby that night, six years before in that very same hospital, and I felt so sorry for my wife. The nurse who met me when I arrived at the neonatal unit told me that just a while after she rang me, our baby started breathing on her own, and her heart was beating again. She recovered slowly but steadily and was discharged after a month or so.

She was a delightful baby and at first it looked as if nothing was wrong with her – she only had some feeding problems. At four months of age we noticed some weakness on her right side. She did not walk until she was three years old and all our neighbours who had known her all her life came to see her taking her first steps. The weakness of her right arm and some weakness of her right leg has been a real handicap to her; she also started with seizures that needed treatment. She had lots of physiotherapy and went to a school for children with cerebral palsy at the beginning. As she did so well academically, she was transferred to an ordinary primary school. Here we learned a lot about how insensitive grown-ups and other children can be towards a child with a handicap. She could not participate in many of the school activities, but she has a lovely voice and enjoyed singing. Just because she could not climb the steps where the choir stood she was left out. She could not carry her school case, so we got her a little cart to put her case on and pull it. Some children always made fun of her by tipping it over and then running away. Hopefully things have changed now.

My wife shed many tears when Linmari was rejected so many times by other children, sometimes they just turned their backs on her while she was still talking to them. She said on a few occasions, "Why was I allowed to live?" However, we pressed on together. She finished school and went to college; she has her own family now and is such a joy and inspiration to us. Frequently she still gets frustrated at not being able to use her right hand. Though she compensates well with her left hand, there are many occasions in daily living where you need two hands. You can quickly find out what they are if you tie one hand behind your back or hold on to something with one hand for a while. As she grew up I learned more about dealing with handicapped patients from her than from what I was taught at medical school.

Because I wanted to spend more time with my family, I sold my practice and took up a teaching position at the university. The paediatrician who took over my practice was a brilliant, hard-working man, who nearly doubled the number of patients I saw. We never knew exactly why, but he later committed suicide. We thought it could have been the stress of the extremely demanding work situation and the demands of his home life. We all felt so sad about such a waste of a good life, and blamed ourselves for not being more available for him to talk to someone about his situation. Another tragic case was that of a student who committed suicide because he thought he had failed his exams, but when the results came he had actually done very well.

Once as a student the thought of suicide did cross my mind. We were in theatre and the patient needed blood very urgently. There was blood ready for her at the blood bank and I ran off to get it. On my way back, I came down some spiral steps ending in a foyer with a hard-wooden floor and in my haste my foot slipped and I fell. The blood was in glass bottles at that time and both the bottles I was carrying broke and the blood spilled all over the floor and all over me. For a moment, I anticipated suicide as I saw myself as a failure who would never be able to become a doctor. Then I thought of the patient in need and about those who depend on me in order to be able to help her. I jumped up, washed myself a bit in a basin, and ran back to the blood bank. On hearing my story, they issued me with two bottles of O Rh negative blood which could be given to almost anybody, and I ran back with it, careful not to slip again. "Thanks" said the anaesthetist and then, "What happened to you?" There was no time to wait for an answer and he started giving the blood immediately to the patient. She did really well and I removed my bloody hospital clothes, showered, and went home in my clean clothes, tired, but alive!

Many times, people give up when they should just give the situation a chance to develop fully or do something about it. When I was young there was a man near us who gassed himself in his car because of 'the hell his wife and mother in law gave him.' I still remember my uncle's words, "Why did he not just 'slide past, take a plane and disappear, rather than kill himself?" I was considering these words later and thought getting on a plane and disappearing sounded irresponsible, but then I thought, he disappeared anyhow, and what memories did he leave? So, it sounded better to me to remove yourself from the situation that is driving you to suicide, if you cannot remove or overcome it. At least you have the chance to come back again later!

Rejection may make people despondent, but overcoming rejection makes one stronger. Therefore, although people suffering from ADHD may have a higher incidence of suicide, the ones who survive may be more resilient than the general population because they have learned to deal with rejection from childhood. I have been rejected on many occasions as long as I can remember, which brings to mind an incident that I can relate to you. I once wrote an essay when I was at school. I did not like homework very much, but when I started writing this essay, I got so excited that I just kept on writing until late that evening – the words just seem to flow. Next day at school the teacher was so impressed with it, I had to read it out for the class. I had an elder brother – bless him, he is not with us anymore – with whom I identified so strongly that I was always talking about him; so much so that on one occasion some boys called me with the words, "Marius come and tell us about your brother!" Anyhow I proudly gave my essay to him to read which he did. He probably wanted to give me honest feedback, his comment was: "I can see it is not your own work, you must have taken it from a book." Books may have inspired me, but this was my own work. I was hurt, but I still loved him and admired him. Thinking back to it now, I should have been flattered that I was able to produce something so extraordinary, that someone could think it was too good to come from me! Later when I was at another school I wrote another essay that the teacher asked me to read out for the class.

On another occasion, I visited a friend who had an accordion, I played a bit on it and was excited that I might be able to play it if I had one to practice on. My dad said he would buy me one and I shared this with my other brother and one of my cousins, as we were sitting in my uncle's study. They told me, "Dad will just waste his money; you will never go on to play it." I thought maybe they were right and told my dad I didn't want one anymore. I never played a musical instrument, though I like singing and am able to remember songs easily.

This second brother of mine was actually a lovely person, very well organised. He became a teacher and then head teacher of a number of schools and before he died he was appointed as an inspector of schools. I think his attitude to life was summarised in the words of this little poem which was on his desk:

Let me live in a house by the side of the road,
Where the race of men go by,

Of men who are good, and men who are bad,
As good and as bad as I,
I will not sit in the scorner's seat,
Or hurl the cynic's ban,
Let me live in a house by the side of the road,
And be a friend to man.
(A verse from The House by the Side of the Road by Sam Walter Foss)

But all he accomplished did not come easily. From a young age he suffered from severe asthma attacks. He could not attend during his last years at school and had to write his exams at home. Because Mum spent so much time with him the two of them were very close. He was one of the first to use a little glass atomizer, where you had to pour a liquid in, called Brovon and the atomizer made it into a spray which you inhaled. He eventually got a bit better when he started these inhalations and did well at college, university and later, until that day when he had a very severe attack when he was in his fifties. My poor sister-in-law was so frightened that she could not get the liquid into the atomizer in time and he died. Maybe it wouldn't have saved him but she suffered from a lot of guilt feelings about this, just like we all do at times when things go wrong. When Linda fell and broke her hip with all the complications that followed, I felt that I should have been there for her because I was already her carer at that time, and she had experienced falls before then. However, we can't turn back the clock and the only thing we can do is to come to terms with it, that we did not do it on purpose, and try not to let it happen again – if there is an again! To be the 'best me' doesn't mean that situations like this won't happen or that we will never make mistakes.

As I was thinking about the co-morbidities of ADHD. I decided that I might have a touch of Asperger's, because I do not mind at all to be on my own and have some problems with relationships.

At conferences, I would many times stand on my own during coffee breaks until I decided to look for someone else on his own, walk over to him and introduce myself. That really solved my problem and I have met many interesting people doing that. Unlike many Asperger's sufferers though, I do have a lot of empathy for others. For instance, I related very well with the parents of my patients, because I made so many mistakes when bringing up my own children.

When I was younger I would do some silly things, maybe more attention-seeking than anything else. At the start of secondary school, all the new pupils had to gather in the school hall, where we got some introductory lessons. One morning it was all about hygiene and the teacher started by saying, "When we bathe we start by washing our faces, isn't that right?" I put up my hand. "Yes?" she said, a little bit annoyed by the interruption.

"I wash my feet first," I said. The whole class erupted in laughter and I got a nick-name which I will better not tell you!

Later, after doing and saying more of these kind of things, the teacher told me, "There is a little boy inside you, who always wants attention; he has to grow up." I did try to take it to heart, but to this day that little boy still comes out now and then! Not that it is always negative – I think many film stars would not have come as far as they did without an element of attention seeking. I also think it contributed my becoming cheerleader of our school at sport events in my senior years. Attention seeking is like pursuing happiness; neither of them can last if they are a primary aim, they are the result of an overwhelming sense of entitlement!

Some of the other co-morbidities I may have include anxiety when feeling insecure or rejected, depression at times and ODD (Oppositional Defiant Disorder). When I was in high school, my parents sent me to a boarding school where I was quite rebellious. Here I was once in the biggest fight of my life. We were in the study hall and this guy said I irritated him and gave me a slap in the face.

That was enough reason for a fight and at the end of study time the boys lined up against the wall of the big bathroom. My friend coached me a bit beforehand. "Look Pottie," he said, "the guy is much taller than you, so don't try to hit his face at first, go full force for his tummy and when he bends down, hit him hard on his nose." It was all over in minutes and with a bleeding nose he shook hands with me. We became good friends and nobody else challenged me for a fight.

I also have problems with motor co-ordination, which was a real handicap to me in sport. For instance, with rugby I was good at running with the ball if I didn't miss catching it, but I was no good at kicking. I am the only person I know who could not only miss the goal posts when kicking, but miss the ball completely, or only skim it with my boot. During one of the games I was kicked in the head and had concussion for a day. I think that also affected my memory, so I do not advise people with attention and memory problems to play contact sports. During the next game, I broke my leg near my ankle and that was the end of my rugby career. I had an operation on the same ankle recently as it became arthritic due to that long-ago injury. In music I could not understand how I could do something like playing the drum in the cadet orchestra for a long time and then for no reason at all get out of rhythm. The same with dancing. In fact consistency has never been my strong point and that has created some problems with the upbringing of our children. Thankfully my wife compensated.

I want to pay tribute to a colleague who, probably more than any other person, was a real inspiration to me in terms of my medical career. His name was Dr J H Erasmus, but for short I will now use his nickname, Rassie, the same as his eldest son, who is also a paediatrician. I had great admiration for him, and he was such a unique person, that I have to be careful not to write the rest of this book about him! Anyhow I hope that many of his patients who are now grown up, will also read it.

When I started working as a Paediatric registrar in 1968, he was running a child guidance clinic at Pretoria academic hospital. I sat in on his clinics and later I saw my own patients at the same clinic. One day when he was sitting in on one of my consultations, he said something like, "You have a natural gift to relate to the children and their parents, which not everyone has." Coming from him, these words were of great encouragement to me. Rassie had two specialist degrees; one in Paediatrics and one in Child Psychiatry. While studying for the second he worked at Maudesly Hospital in London. During this time, a few youngsters kept on throwing stones onto the roof of his house. One evening he had just had enough. As he started to run after them, they scattered in all directions, so he decided to run after just one of them and, as he was catching up with him, the little guy kept shouting at the top of his voice, "Why pick on me? Why pick on me?" Anyhow he showed Rassie where he lived, and he took him home to his parents and never had problems again. The others must have thought next time it would be one of them!

This is how I knew Rassie, full of zest and always having a solution to a problem. It is from him that I learned that if you work hard at your surgery during the day and come home late in the evening, the only time you have left to dictate reports to the GPs who referred the patients is at 5 am. This I have done all my work life. I am sure he wanted me to become a child psychiatrist. He gave me books to read to inspire me but he never said anything. However, I wouldn't let go of being a paediatrician. When I saw children with really difficult behaviour problems, I sometimes wished that he had given me more of a push. On the other hand, a paediatric approach, even to behaviour problems is different. A child psychiatrist once told me: "Marius why are you so worried? There will always be patients you can't help." I know he was right, but that was not my approach. As paediatrician, I was more accustomed to have to act in acute situations, where something just had to be done. The downside is that in behavioural paediatrics we may be inclined to resort to prescribing medication sooner. At St Peter's I worked in paediatrics and also with child psychiatrists, and later developed a Paediatric Psychiatry approach, which is somewhere between the two disciplines.

Rassie had two farms, a small one a few miles outside Pretoria where the family home was and a large game farm in the Thabazimbi area. We regularly took children from the clinic to both these farms. There they had freedom from the restricted life of a city home. On his smaller farm, he had an old double decker bus, and they could sleep in there or outside anywhere, though Rassie kept the swimming pool gate locked shut outside swimming times, and only he had a key. On both farms, we had a camp fire at night. There was a big plough disk used as a wok and for the evening meal he would first 'braai' sausage and then add about thirty eggs, mix with a wooden spoon and then dish it out the children, who ate it together with maize porridge. They loved it. We took bigger groups to the game farm, together with student Psychologists and Occupational therapists, who mixed with the children. There were many activities including swimming in the farm dam and going game hunting with Rassie on a lorry.

At home at the weekends he would regularly do his ward rounds on horseback. He had a great sense of humour and could get away with saying things for which others would be frowned upon. For instance, he admitted a baby to the hospital with the surname of Fokine, which apparently is a well-known Russian surname. Anyhow he made use of the opportunity to call the ward and ask how the Fokine baby was. During that time, it was taboo to use the F word, not like today. He told me later how the nurses handled it so graciously, by adding an l to the baby's name while he was in hospital, so when he came and wanted to pester the nurses, there at the end of his cot appeared the name Folkine.

We had many situations at the clinic where you had to keep a straight face at all costs. There was a couple who always brought their child to us. The woman was big and tall and the man short and skinny. She did the talking, he never said a word. One day she brought the child on her own. "Where is Uncle Johnny?" asked Rassie.
"Oh doctor," she said, "he is no more with us."
"So sorry to hear that, what happened to him?"
"He touched a live wire and was electrocuted..." and then as if an afterthought, "and it wasn't even a strong current, doctor!"

At one-time Rassie applied for the position of Head of the Paediatric department, but someone else got the job. I always felt that was a pity, as I think Rassie would have infused the department with his enthusiasm, hard work and leadership. He also had strong convictions, but if you did not know him well, you will probably not have noticed it in his daily conduct, as he had such a jovial and outgoing personality. He put very high demands on himself and I never heard him blaming others.

I want to to mention Ria, Rassie's wife, who is such a loveable, efficient and supportive person. There was always an atmosphere of serenity in their home, for which Ria was responsible. She was also the one who mowed their large lawn with a ride-on mower and I suppose did many other things I do not know about. Anyhow whenever I visited them they always had time for me and I got the feeling that everything was under control.

There was another paediatrician whom I admired, and that was Dr Alet Haasbroek – the one who ventilated Linmari by hand all night. She was very strict on the parents of her patients, but they still came to her from long distances because she was so good. She had a lot of experience with the treatment of patients suffering from diabetes. Once she went on holiday and asked me to stand in for. I had just finished with my specialist training and started my own private practice. I have to admit that diabetes wasn't my particular interest. My receptionist came in to tell me about the next patient. "These people came all the way from a neighbouring country with the expectation to see Dr Haasbroek, because their child's diabetes is so difficult to treat that their doctors can't help him. They seem to be very knowledgeable about their child's illness, and the father has a notebook with lots of questions for you."

The parents came in with their son who was nine years old. "Dr, we are so glad to see you, we came to see Dr Haasbroek, but your receptionist assured us you will be able to help us just as well, as she otherwise wouldn't have asked you to stand in for her!"

Needless to say, I could not answer quite a few of their questions. My best solution was to keep my poise, examine the child, write down their concerns carefully, and tell them, "Rather than rushing it, I will write a full report, and send it to you." Of course, this would give me enough time to do research.

The receptionist told me later. "You looked worried when I told you about them, but those parents were really impressed!"

I was also privileged to have had Dr Madel van Dyk as my associate in the paediatric practice at Unitas Hospital in Centurion. She was first a pharmacist, then studied medicine and paediatrics and also became a paediatric cardiologist. She brought new vigour in our practice and was the one who kept an eye on our practice finances. One thing among many I learned from her was what one of her teachers always said, "If a thing is not right it is wrong!"

At the end of 1982 our family decided to sell our house and get rid of our furniture and other belongings that we wouldn't need and went off to join YWAM (Youth with a mission) in Hawaii. The base was on the big island at a place called Kailua Kona.

I actually wanted to work on their mercy ship called Anastasis, but it was in for refurbishment when we came there, and we stayed on the island and went on healthcare outreaches to other places. While we were there, I gave lectures to the healthcare team and went twice with them to Guatemala. The experiences I had there during a turbulent time in the history of the country are enough to cover at least a chapter of a book, but I will just tell a few.

We collected medicines donated to us in San Antonio Texas where the team worked with the ambulance crews for a while to get first-hand experience of medical emergencies. The team members stayed with people in different private homes and the family I stayed with lend me one of their cars to drive to the ambulance station every evening and back to their home in the early hours of the morning. I am great in getting lost and this is exactly what happened to me on my way back, the first night. I had no idea where I was and parked under a street light in the road to look at a map I had with me – there would be no other cars around at 3 am, so I thought. I had scarcely stopped, however, when a police car pulled up next to me with a flashing red light and a policeman got out. I opened the window.

"What are you doing here this time of the night and why do you park on the street corner?" I tried to explain but I could see on his face that he did not believe me. "Go off," he said, and that is what I did, but I was still lost! I drove around for a while and then decided to stop again to look at the map, under a street lamp but as far as possible to the side of the street. I did not realise I had driven in a circle and this was the same place. I had hardly stopped and there was the red light again!

"Get out," said the policeman, "and put both your hands on the roof of your car."

It was winter and I stood there shivering, with only my white doctor's coat on as protection against the cold. I assume he thought that was all part of my 'made up' story. I said, "The inside lamp of the car isn't…" But he did not give me a chance to tell him the light wasn't working and that was why I was parked under the street lamp. Parking again under the same lamp after had had warned me the first time had understandably annoyed him.

"I put it to you that you have stolen this car. Whose car, is it?"

"It belongs to Mr Lyon."

"Ha!" he said, and I thought I heard him mumble," Doctor from South Africa with a lion's car? What a story!" He went to his car and checked on the number plate. It was still in name of the previous owner, not on that of Chris Lyon. I pictured myself in jail as he approached me with handcuffs, but as I fumbled in my pocket I found a piece of paper with Chris' telephone number on it. The policeman went back to his car to phone the number and came back with a completely different attitude. "Sorry doctor" he said. "Get into your car and I will escort you to Mr Lyon's home!"

At that time, 1983, Mexico did not allow white South Africans into their country, not even in transit. So, as the rest of the team went from San Antonio through Mexico by train, I went by plane with eighty boxes of medicine. Getting them through customs at the other end, where they only spoke Spanish, took three days.

I still had to be licenced to work as doctor in Guatemala. In America, I had to pass an examination, but here they referred me to the son of the president. I came to his office, explained to him where I came from and that we want to set up clinics in the rural areas of his country. He called out something to someone in the office next door, who brought a stamp with an ink pad. He stamped my passport and signed it. It said: "Licence to practice Medicine in Guatemala." (Translated from Spanish) That was it.

We stayed amongst people who lived under awful circumstances in Indian villages in the mountains where we offered medical help at clinics that we set up in burned down schools, churches or even outside.

50

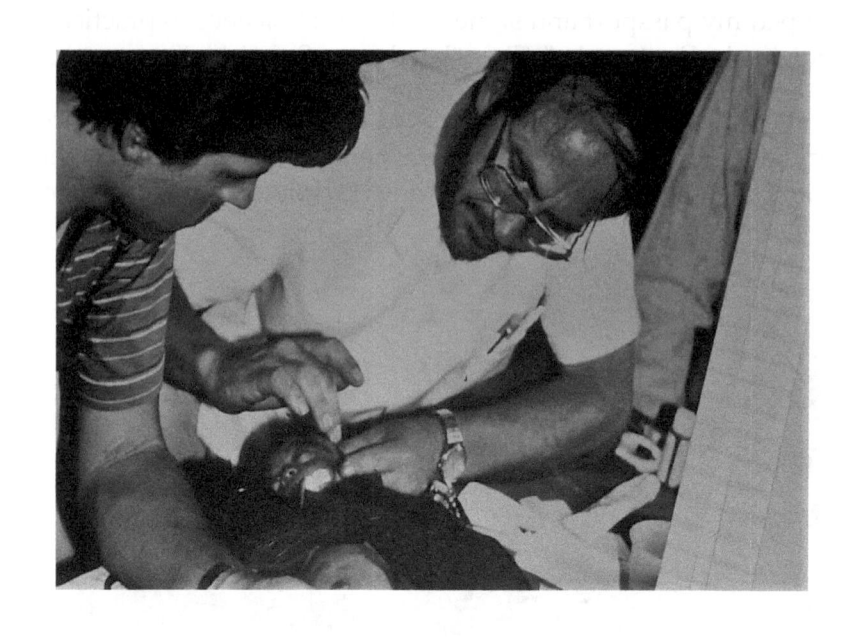

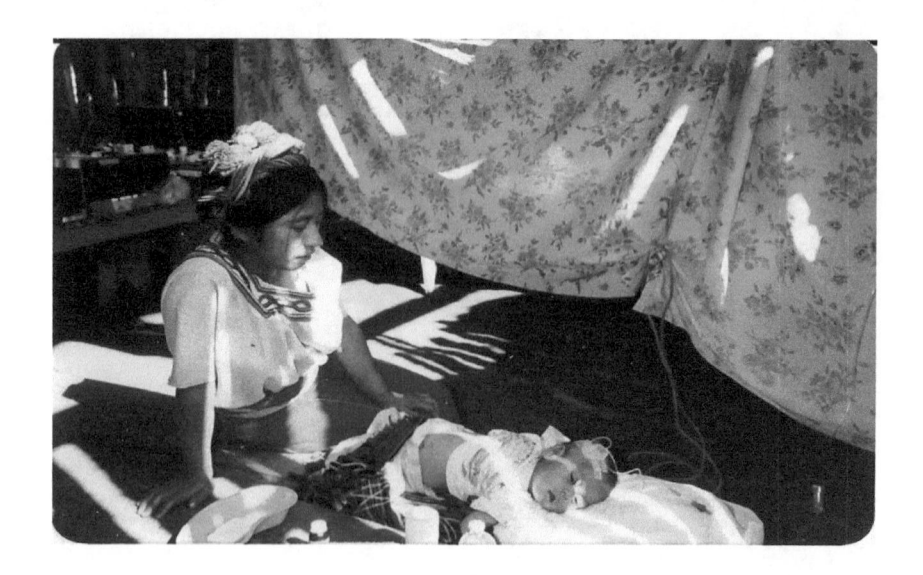

On the photo on the previous page paramedic Don Traller and I were putting up a scalp vein infusion on a dehydrated baby. The people were very grateful for our help. Some of the team members stayed behind to continue helping the people with health care, after we left.

While I was there I contracted scabies, a skin disease caused by a small bug that creeps under your skin and itches terribly. There are medications to put on your skin but you also have to get rid of them from your clothes. I had bought myself quite an expensive tracksuit, which I wore regularly, and I was convinced that this had become infested. The only way to get rid of the bug was to put your clothes in boiling water for a few minutes. I explained it to the lady who helped with the cooking, gave her the tracksuit and went off to the clinic. When I returned after about three hours, I found that my communication with her hadn't worked; there was my track suit in the pot with boiling water on the fire! It had shrunk from top to bottom. I even hung stones on it, but nothing could save it.

Our team comprised two paramedics and two nurses from the USA, another nurse and a chiropractor from Australia, a few others and myself as the doctor. We saw more than a hundred patients per day, and of course referred all our patients with backache to Jonathan, our chiropractor! Good team work and friendship was absolutely necessary. There was one night that I will never forget. By this time Jonathan and I had become great friends and, when he contracted diarrhoea, he woke me up asking me to please accompany him to the toilet that was about fifty yards from where we were sleeping. That was OK, but there was a lot of terrorist activity in the area and by night they came down from the mountains to the villages and might shoot at anyone around. We took off all our white clothing, because that made us easy targets, leopard-crawled to the toilet and fortunately got back safely. That was a scary experience, but we were even better friends afterwards. I remembered I once heard Jim Rohn saying, "A friend is someone who will do anything for you." He said, "If for some reason they put me in jail in Mexico and they allow me to phone my friend in California in the middle of the night, he will not hesitate to get in his car and come and bail me out." I also heard someone say you should at least have eight friends and near family members to carry the coffin at your funeral!

Coming back to Guatemala, I had an experience when I really thought I was going crazy. We had to go to a Spanish school for a crash course in Spanish. The others prepared for it by studying basic Spanish, but I thought I would just learn it at the school, so when I entered the room where a lady tutor was waiting for me I hardly knew more than just a few words of the language The tutor did not know a single word in English. After four hours of misunderstandings, I became so anxious and frustrated that I jumped up and walked out of the school into the street. All the homes had entrance doors in one long wall. In my disturbed state of mind, I walked up and down the street trying to find the door to the home where I was staying. What made it worse was that while I did this people in the street laughed at me – I knew it was at me because I constantly heard one word I knew, "Gringo" their slang word for an obvious foreigner. I felt some rejection creeping in, though I am sure they were just joking. Standing up to rejection had never been my strong point. I decided just to stand there beside the street and tried to relax a bit. At least I thought that nobody will be able to make a joke of me.

"¿Cómo estás?" I knew what that meant!

"Estoy bien," I lied, but when he started talking, I did not understand a word that he was saying. Anyhow, he was from the school and took me to the right door.

A military junta was running Guatemala at the time, following a coup the previous year. Four guerrilla groups had merged to make themselves stronger and the country was in a state of civil war with the civilians, as always, bearing the brunt. When they heard there was medical help available, many of our patients came down from the mountains where they had escaped, after being driven from their homes by guerrilla fighters. Our team was sometimes escorted by army vehicles and one day the vehicle behind was destroyed by a guerrilla attack.

While we were doing clinics, my wife, Linda (*lovely in Spanish*) helped at an orphanage, called Aqua Viva on the outskirts of Guatemala City. We brought children that we found after their parents were killed to the orphanage. Some of them were in a very poor nutritional state.

Not that I condone child labour, but even children who had to work hard were still happy

In spite of all the fighting and hardships, we found more joy amongst the people in Guatemala than in the United States or many other first world countries.

Once on my way from Guatemala to Hawaii I had to stay over in Los Angeles for a connecting flight. I only had Guatemalan money with me and they refused to exchange it for dollars at the airport. I went through my pockets and found only one American quarter, with this I decided to phone David, a young man with whom I had become acquainted in Hawaii. His mother answered the phone and said David wasn't there.

"Please!" I nearly shouted when I gathered she was going to put the phone down, "don't put down the phone!" I mentioned that I made the phone call with the only money I had, and explained my situation. She established where to find me at the airport, came and picked me up and took me to furnished apartment, for which she was the estate agent, after getting some groceries along the way. She told me I could stay until I got my connecting flight, which was booked for two days' time. As she left she turned around and gave me one hundred dollars.

"A man should not be without money," she said!

Wasn't that cool?

The next morning, I was preparing breakfast with the groceries David's mum had bought me, when there was a knock on the door. I thought maybe it was someone interested in the flat, but there, right before me, was Jannie Truter from my hometown of Pretoria.

"How on earth did you find me here?"

"David told me. But there is no time to waste, I hear you are only going to Hawaii tomorrow, so let's get going!" Behind him in the street was an impressive motorbike which he had rented for the day. I forgot about my breakfast and we went to lots of places including Hollywood, driving along the Sunset Boulevard, downtown Los Angeles and the Pier. I saw all this from the back seat of a motorbike. And all of it for a quarter!

While we were in Hawaii Andre, who had stayed behind in South Africa to finish school, arrived to complete our family. This photo of us all – Johan, Linda, Andre, Linmari and Marius – was taken in 1983. At the time of writing (2017) there are sixteen grandchildren and four great grandchildren. All starting with the love of two people and their commitment to each other in 1963.

We stayed at the YWAM base on Hawaii for more than a year. Here we regularly met people from lots of different countries. Our transport was the "London bus" that ran up and down the coast and was free to go on, being sponsored by the seaside hotels. We sometimes hitchhiked. During the time here, I only wore shorts and sandals.

Before we went back to South Africa, we returned to Jim and Cecilia Leininger whom we had met in San Antonio and helped on their retreat ranch. As I was not registered in America as a doctor I did the odd jobs, mainly in the garden, and looked after the cattle. Linda looked after the guests, but also helped me at times. Apart from encounters with scorpions, wasps and fire-ants, we had a big scare one day with the cattle. Linda was putting their food in a crib and I went slightly up the hill and whistled for them to come. I started to walk back to where Linda was when I saw her throw down the feed shouting, "They are coming!" and start running. When I looked back I saw what she meant – about twenty cows and a bull were coming over the hill at a speed and I was between them and their food! I ran so fast I even left my sandals behind!

57

We returned to South Africa where I worked again for a number of years as paediatrician. During this time, I learnt a very expensive lesson. Apart from my paediatric practice, we started a guesthouse and then opened another one. When my wife was able to manage them, things went well, but after she got injured, we had to get other people in to run them and things went downhill. I was too busy to give them my attention and just had to put money into the project until I could do it no longer. At this stage the interest on our mortgages doubled and at the end I had to sell everything for peanuts with a great financial loss from, which I could not recover. If I had not ventured into things I wasn't trained for, this would not have happened. The same thing happened later when I bought diamonds with the money we made selling our home in 1982 before we went to Hawaii. Diamond prices fell by a third soon afterwards and I remember walking up and down the streets of Honolulu to try and sell my diamonds for what I paid for them, without success. All this happened because I did not stick to what I could do best, invest my money safely and not take risks. We have bought and sold quite a number of houses in our lifetime and would have done very well if we had only invested the profits we made from one house into the next and not spent the money on other schemes.

When I went to visit my brother in the UK, he mentioned a paediatric post being advertised. I applied for it and, during the first months of 2002, I was appointed clinical fellow in the Department of Paediatrics at St Peter's Hospital, Chertsey. It felt to me like a new beginning, with all the excitement that newness brings. Winter was saying farewell and nature was reviving. I still remember the trees with little white flowers along the road.

Linda and I got a one bedroom flat in the staff accommodation and really enjoyed staying there. We moved to a bigger place with four bedrooms when our daughter and her two children joined us. It was close to the hospital and easy to get to work and back. One of my precious memories is of my granddaughter and me, early on Saturday mornings, racing one other to the central laundry, each carrying a bag of clothes. In the front garden of the building were many wild rabbits. The children enjoyed looking at them and thought they were cute. To show how our priorities may differ, we told a friend with a vegetable garden about the rabbits and on his face, we could see that he did not like rabbits, he said that he tried to get rid of them for the sake of his vegetables.

St Peter's is a really big hospital and adjusting was quite a challenge to me, as it was different in many ways from what I was used to. For instance they used generic names for medicines where I was used to the trade names, and there were many set guidelines for treating conditions where I was used to do things my way, but I managed to survive. I was working in the A&E, children's wards, neonatal unit and outpatients all at the same time, as well as attending caesarean sections and looking after the babies in the maternity unit at short notice. At first, I got lost a few times due to my poor sense of direction. I noticed a few things that tickled me; one was in the dining room/kitchen of the neonatal unit. The nurses put up a notice above the sink, obviously directed at the doctors: "If you have not arranged with your mother to do your washing up, please do it yourself." And in the doctors meeting room there were two circles drawn against the wall, the one below the other. In the top one was written "If you become frustrated, bump your head here!" And in the lower circle, "If you are short, bump it here!"

I soon experienced the value of a good icebreaker. It was just after I started to work at the hospital that the Paediatric Department came together at a farewell function for a doctor who had worked there for many years and was now retiring. Everyone was talking over cakes and beverages. The head of the department gave a short farewell speech and, after the applauding stopped with everybody in good spirits, he suddenly turned to me, "Marius tell us a South African joke!" It became quiet as all eyes turned to me when I got up. This was unexpected and thoughts about what to say rushed through my mind. "Well" I thought "I will just tell this one as well as I can." On this day, I fortunately did not experience a word-finding problem, like I do have sometimes, especially when stressed, that is why I would rather write than speak – it gives me more time to think. Anyhow I started to say that there are quite a few of us (I for instance was over sixty years old at that time) who are "Running to catch retirement, but only this doctor has made it."

It was still quiet as I continued, "It makes me think about the three men who were running to catch a train, just as it pulled out of the station. All three of them were running as fast as they could. At last one of them caught the train and was off. The two who missed the train, instead of feeling sad just started laughing. Someone who saw the whole thing said to them, 'How can you two be laughing at your friend who at least got on the train which you missed?' Still laughing one of them answered, 'Yes, but he came to see us off!'"
That was the right joke for the right occasion, and it opened my way in the department. Because of this I was even asked to be Santa for the siblings of the babies in the neonatal unit. I had to practise real hard at "HO, HO, HO!"

Because of my background and experience I could sometimes function on a more senior level than my contemporaries. For instance, in my practice I did many lumbar punctures, and I could help out when one of the other doctors who did not have that much experience got stuck. But when I had the opportunity to become a consultant, I did not present myself convincingly enough on paper to get on the register. This was because of my tendency not to give enough attention to detail – a problem I had also experienced when I worked on my MD thesis. This was before I took medication. (Concerta) One of the advantages of taking the medication, apart from being more focused, was that it was not so difficult and boring to give attention to detail. It also got easier throughout the day and I could now stay awake even during meetings where I usually went to sleep. The downside was that I was not able to take refreshing power naps during the day and had difficulty going to sleep at night. I also felt anxious and down during many late afternoons, but taking into account that I was able to be much more productive during working hours, without over-exerting myself, the medication was worthwhile to me.

After I retired, I stopped the medication, not needing to perform so much as at work, and able to relax during the day when needed.

I feel less tense and happier in myself without the medication, though I still take it when I have to drive longer distances. By this I experienced first-hand that ADHD is to some extent a product of modern living practices, especially the school/work situations and the demands we are subjected to. There are, however, still other aspects which also improve with medication, like relationships – the person on medication will be able to listen better to what the other person has to say.

One incident I remember when working with children with behaviour problems, mostly patients with ADHD, at St Peter's Hospital, was when a boy of about 14 who was brought to me one day by the officer involved with the children of travellers. This boy was very rebellious and nasty towards others. As I talked to him and looked at him, I saw him as a child who had serious emotional hurts in his life. He acted out of his feelings of loneliness and insecurity. In the past, we would name it 'burnt child syndrome.' I felt so sorry for him, that for the second time in my 'doctor life' I started to cry. When I could speak again, he asked me, "Doctor, why were you crying?"
"Because I sensed how much you are hurting inside." At the next consultation, he brought his sister and some of his other family members with him to show them 'the doctor who cried about me.' He is grown up now, but he will know I am talking about him if he may read this.

She was about thirteen years old when her parents brought her to our behaviour clinic. Let's call her Sarah. Her life unfolded before me as I listened to her and her parents, read reports from her teachers, and looked at the results of some tests I had done; e.g. The Connors questionnaire. Everyone stated that she could be a bright young girl, but inconsistently so. That, she said, made her feel unsure of herself; she never knew when she was not able to do something simple that less clever children could do, and this made her feel stupid. In class, she was daydreaming a lot, it seemed that her thoughts would just go astray, but nobody else seem to notice it, she felt like she was carrying a burden all alone. She could not understand what was wrong with her, and nobody else could understand why she did not finish tasks, resented homework, and her room was always in a mess. She got quite depressed about the situation, but still suffered in silence. Socially, though she was very chatty, she had problems with the subtler nuances of social interaction, and she was ridiculed by other girls when she made inappropriate remarks, or became over talkative, or lost the thread of the conversation. At some stage, she self-harmed by cutting, which brought temporary relief of her anxiety. She had started to enjoy attention from older boys who were clearly going to take advantage of her; this bothered her parents more than anything else at that stage. She had also started smoking secretly and the mother thought she had once smelled weed in her room. Her story was typically that of a girl with ADHD. There are books addressing the treatment of girls and women with ADHD, I will just touch on it in part 2. Some of my most difficult patients to treat were girls. I remember one girl who was so rebellious that she was excluded from school, except for Wednesdays when she was the star of the football team. She could kick a ball so hard that it once broke the arm of the goal keeper!

An interesting observation I have made through the years is that you can be popular and successful at one place and just the opposite at another. I experienced it when I did locums for paediatricians who had their practices in different towns. In the one place, all went well but in another I just didn't function as I was used to, and even had to call in the help of a less experienced colleague at one time. I noted that this did not only happen to me. I do not suggest that you should run away from your problems, but if you work at a place where you are accepted and enjoy your work, before you make a change be very sure that it is the right and necessary thing. If, however, things go against you all the time, there may be a better place to be. This is advice for exceptional circumstances, don't make a habit of it, and try not to leave your job before you are sure of the next. One thing I can say about the ten years I worked at St Peters Hospital, either in the department of paediatrics or when I did sessions at the child and adolescent mental health care services (CAMHS), there was not a single day that anybody made me feel unwelcome.

Before I end Part One, I would still like to tell you a crocodile story. When I explained the use of medication to my younger patients, I told them to have ADHD is like swimming in a pool with crocodiles. You could try to swim away from them, but they will probably catch up with you. Medication is like shooting them with hard rubber bullets, it will keep them away for a while and give you a chance to get to the other side. Sometimes they get out of the water and chase you like this.

The picture was drawn by my grandson when he was twelve

Crocodiles make me think of a story Felix Masinjira Mashedi once told...

There was a man who started with very little, but worked very hard and at the end of the day, had a formidable business empire with many employees. He had an impressive home with a swimming pool inside. One day he announced that he wanted to appoint a second-in-command and for this occasion he invited all his employees to his home. He took them to his swimming pool and as they were gathering around it, they were astonished to see two crocodiles swimming around in it. The man started to speak:
"Many of you know the hardships I had to overcome to be where I am today, so I want my second-in-command to be a man of the same calibre. Therefore, anyone who can jump into this swimming pool today and swim through to the other side will have the position of being second-in command with immediate effect.
Everyone was looking at each other, then suddenly the most junior chap was in the pool. He swam very fast with a spray of water around him, and then he shot out on the other side with the crocodiles' jaws snapping at his heels.
The man called him and said, "Because of what you did just now, you are officially second under me. Anything you want to say?"
"Yes" said the young man. "I have one question."
"And what is that?" asked the man.
"Who pushed me?"

Relating what others have said about me; in spite of all the shortcomings I grew up with, I have been a good doctor and paediatrician. I had great colleagues to work with, one whom, Dr Wajdi Nackasha, is very near to the ideal paediatrician. He has become one of my best friends. I loved my patients, and when I retired, some of them just did not want to go to another doctor.

After my retirement from medicine in 2011, I still kept my interest in ADHD going. I became a full-time carer for my wife Linda, who has become disabled and also suffers from dementia. My lovely wife who had always been so creative… The two of us cannot have much of a conversation anymore, but she understands it well when I kiss her and tell her that she is still my sweetheart.

I am now seventy-eight, my motto the same, and I offer you the message of this book to decide for yourself if you want to say:

I will always try to be,
THE BEST ME I CAN BE.

Though I am now going to teach you in Part Two about being organised, make time to relax, otherwise your life will become one long nightmare of work. That is not what I want for you. Like giving to others, you should not do it grudgingly, give with a cheerful heart. See being a fulfilled and organised person, as a gift you can give to yourself and those around you. Don't try to be someone else, just a better you. To quote Jim Rohn again, "Look after yourself for me, and I will look after myself for you."

The book is here to help you be joyful, positive and fulfilled,
not sad, negative and frustrated.

Part two

69 Foreword
72 The Heart of the Matter
82 Knowing my limits
83 Planning and Organising
100 Overcoming Poor Concentration
104 Developing Memory Power
108 Driving with AD
112 Suicide
114 Motor Co ordination
115 Perception
117 Specific Learning Disorders
119 Developing and Keeping Momentum
129 Money Management
133 Healthy Relationships
142 Overcoming Feelings of Failure
148 A Final Word

150 Appendix One
157 Appendix Two
161 Appendix Three

163 Useful Resources
166 Copyright Law and Legal Disclaimer

Foreword

Everyone has, at some time, experienced problems with concentration that eventually affect finances, lifestyle, ambitions, and family. This lack of concentration and attention is accentuated during stressful situations, thereby leading to more stress. This results in a vicious circle of stress and lack of attention. Usually when the stressful situation passes, concentration improves, except if there is a physiological cause for the poor concentration and inability to sustain attention.

It has been my experience through the years that stress is alleviated when I realise that there is only one person I can be, and that is me. So why not try to make the best of me in all situations? I cannot really do more than my best, except by delegating particular issues to someone better equipped to deal with them.

This urge to share the best approaches and warn against the not-so-effective approaches motivated me to write this book.

'I WILL BE THE BEST ME I CAN BE' was originally based on the adult part of my book "I HAVE ADHD/ADD – so what? A guide for Teens and Adults" Though there are still similarities, Part 1 was added and Part 2 edited and updated. It is concise, easy to read and simple to apply. The checklists at the end of each chapter can be used easily to assess the progress you have made in improving your executive ability. Award yourself a 2 for the best you can do and a 1 for second best. Try to turn the 1s into 2s. Aim for the best, but be happy with what *you* can achieve. Nobody is perfect.

I see myself as someone standing by you, but you should only take from me, from others and from your own experience, that which you need to live your own unique life.

Remember there are many successful people who have used ADHD to their advantage. Lack of concentration for instance, enhances lateral thinking and improves problem solving abilities in some situations. There is also a positive side to impulsivity.

Turn the *negative* into positive.
Aggression → creativity
Inattention → lateral thinking and problem solving.
→Multitasking
→Imagination
Hyperactivity → work speed and volume
→High energy level
→Risk taking (Positive aspects)

Some of the stories in Part One are there to help you understand and remember what is presented in Part Two. I will mostly leave it to the reader to make the associations – with just the occasional pointer.

Suggestions on how to use the book

- Read it through without trying to remember anything;
- Either commit yourself to continue to use the book or get rid of it and forget about me;
- Read again the parts you may want to understand and remember. Use a pencil to write a 1 or a 2 in the check list boxes provided;
- Implement what is suggested in the book;
- Go through all the check lists once a month and where you are able to, replace 1s with 2s until there are no 1s left!
- Do the same for the final check list weekly, maybe on a Wednesday?
- Do this consistently, so the guidelines of the book become alive in your subconscious;
- Read through the relevant parts of the book a few times to relate the items on the lists to the reasons behind them – or this will just become a sterile box-ticking exercise;
- Use the blank spaces left on the pages to write down your own thoughts or information from other books or speakers – the book is yours!

The Heart of the Matter

This book is the product of my experience of living with the disorder of ADHD and also working with people affected by it. As you are going through the learning process, you will be enabled to help others as well. Helping others will make you stronger. But remember you can only really teach someone else what you understand yourself.

My motive in writing this book has been the urge to help people make their lives more ordered and fulfilling. It becomes difficult for a person affected by an attention deficit disorder to conduct their life, including involvement at home, performance of their job, and working towards their personal objectives. If a thing does not work out this time, do it differently next time. If it does work out, try to do it even better next time!

The advice I will give you in the following pages is based on both my experience as a doctor and my experience as a subject. It utilizes motivational techniques that have been proven to work both for my patients and myself. Understanding what your problem may be goes a far way to help you to overcome it. As I can only teach others what I understand myself, the diagram of the wheel and my explanation of it is how I understand the intricacies of our executive functions.

Understanding the Executive Functions

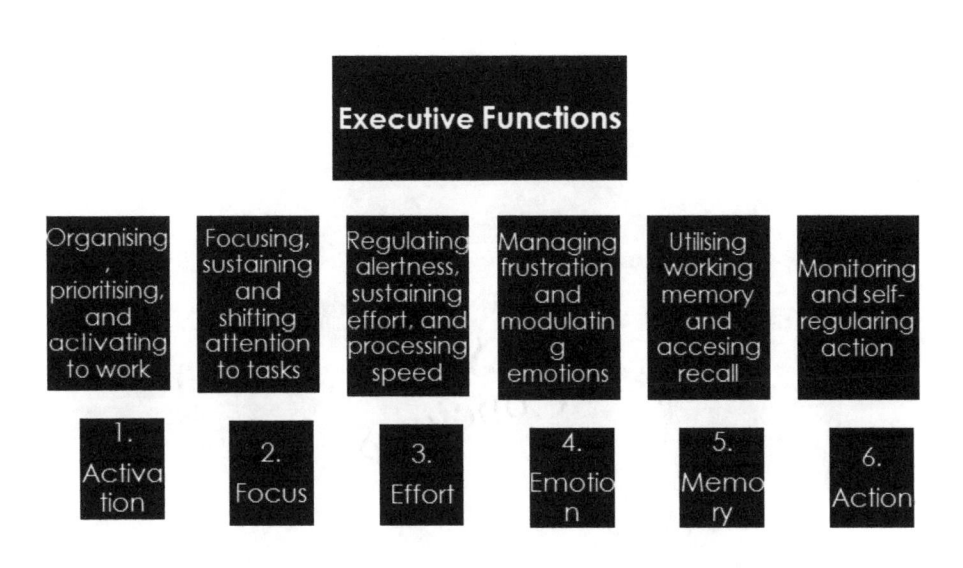

Executive Functions

Organising, prioritising, and activating to work	Focusing, sustaining and shifting attention to tasks	Regulating alertness, sustaining effort, and processing speed	Managing frustration and modulating emotions	Utilising working memory and accessing recall	Monitoring and self-regulating action
1. Activation	2. Focus	3. Effort	4. Emotion	5. Memory	6. Action

This diagram was taken from the book of Dr Thomas Brown:
Attention Deficit Disorder: The Unfocused Mind in Children and Adults

This wheel is how I understand it...

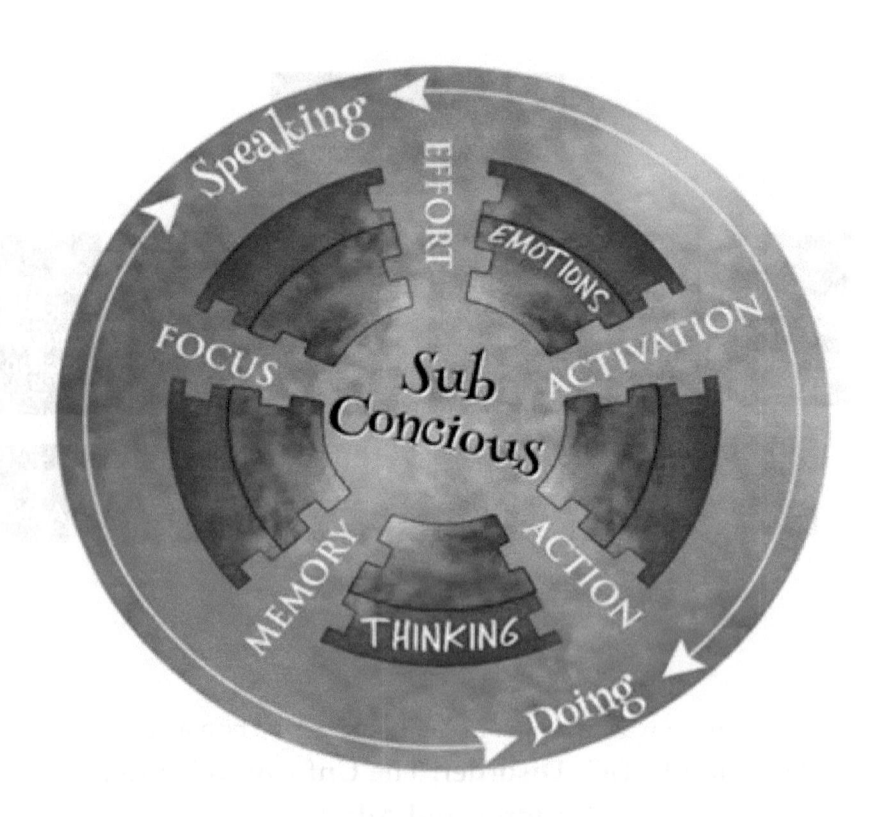

74

There is a team at work within us called 'executive functions'. Each team member, of which there are six, has a particular function.

They are:

1. Activation 2. Focus 3. Effort 4. Emotion 5. Memory 6. Action

There is another way to look at how we function, which is incorporated in the diagram:
1. Think, imagine
2. Say, write or draw
3. Do things and develop healthy habits

Together, subconsciously, the executive functions working in harmony become an inner manager. There is an effect on our emotions and conscious thinking, speaking and doing. Though we do not think about them specifically, we practise them all the time. When something is wrong or doesn't function as it should in our life, we can look at the EFs individually to try and find the 'blockage.'

The wheel demonstrates in a simplified way the connections there are between the conscious and the subconscious and how the executive functions cross from one into the other. Because emotions are so important, I have allocated a special place for them next to the subconscious. Will-power forms part of all the EF together and also of their conscious control. Our emotions may be triggered by our senses and by our thoughts; however, these emotional responses are modulated by previous experiences stored in our subconscious mind. If we can extract these experiences from our subconscious to our conscious memory, this will cause us to understand why we respond in a certain way and bring healing to our minds. It may not be easy to find these unconscious memories, but there are ways to try and do so. Thinking about experiences that may have caused unpleasant memories or speaking to someone you confide in, or even when you are alone and able to 'act them out', do so.

Many times, unpleasant experiences, may cause irrational memories and behaviour. The attempt to overcome these irrational thought processes and behaviour patterns with rational thinking is the idea behind Cognitive Behaviour Therapy (CBT). There is truth in the saying, "don't let your feelings run away with you" or "hijack" you. Try to nip unhealthy emotions in the bud, before they lead, for instance to a rage-attack. Or try to steer them into a more constructive outlet, like walking, or running, some other activity or a punch ball – not a live one! Aggressive feelings may lead to constructive activity if you are able to steer them.

Think of your subconscious as your 'genius self', which remembers your past goals, dreams, and aspirations for the future. Remember that you are still the boss with overall responsibility. By using rational will power one is able to modulate behaviour on the conscious level, but this will have only a limited effect on the subconscious level. As one proceeds with an activity it may, however sink into the subconscious if repeated with consistency. Without the 'inner power' or feeling to accompany the rational will to do things, it's hard to keep motivating oneself and life becomes a struggle. You actually need to put in an enormous amount of energy to keep yourself motivated and focused on the task. It is like turning a clock without a spring or power mechanism with your finger, as soon as you stop doing it, the clock stops. The subconscious parts of your executive functions have to support the conscious parts and if they are properly open, you are on your way to developing integrity. Look at the picture of the wheel and try to think which EF in your situation may have an obstruction and think of ways to remove it or get someone or a professional to help you do so.

For instance, in the picture below, there is a partial obstruction of the EF '**focus**.' This has a detrimental effect on your ability to concentrate. You can remove the obstruction by an increase of neurotransmitters, which I have discussed elsewhere. Medically speaking, the solution to this problem would be to increase the levels of neurotransmitters in the areas of the brain that support executive functions. The fact of the matter is that attention deficit persons have lower levels of neurotransmitters than the levels needed for the appropriate functioning of all executive powers.

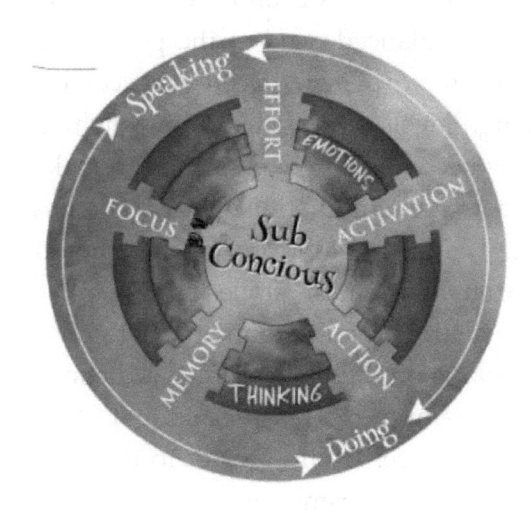

One can to some extent help the brain to overcome these shortcomings. Exercise, or the reception of exciting visual or auditory stimuli can raise the level of neurotransmitters in a

77

person with or without ADHD. Even memories or fantasies about these experiences can induce elevated levels of these internal stimulants. I have read someone say ADD stands for Adventure Deficit Disorder, which has some truth in it.

One needs to maintain the levels by regularly giving stimuli. However, one has to be mindful of the proportion. The production of neurotransmitters (especially dopamine) in the body may have an addictive effect. If one type of stimulus is allowed to develop out of proportion, it affects the balanced need of the person for other stimuli. For instance, if a person receives excessive stimulation (and produces high levels of dopamine) by watching pornography, the subject may become addictive, which can make it very difficult to find other activities stimulating enough, and has an overall negative impact. The story I told on page 8 should encourage you to follow your dreams, but the stones I threw in the dam are like stimuli to release neurotransmitters and the big stones that made the nasty splash-marks on the wall are like addictions that consume your energy and empty the reserves so that other stones cannot cause a surge anymore. Adding water to the dam restores your natural supply of neurotransmitters.

Another illustration of the dopamine surge of an overpowering stimulus is the 'trampoline effect'. If you jump on a trampoline and then get off, your body feels as if the power of gravity has been increased many times, and immediately afterwards it is difficult for you to jump higher than a few inches from the ground.

General excitement and enthusiasm about life (the adventure factor), a balanced physical exercise program, a healthy diet and enough sleep, in *the* other words a *healthy lifestyle, will go a long way towards increasing release of neurotransmitters.*

Talking for a moment about physical exercise, you can jog, or walk, go to the gym or play sport, but there are also a few things you can easily do at home to keep you in shape. Whenever you walk, at home and at work, walk upright with a spring in your step – not awkward, but not sloppy. If you have a pedometer you will be surprised how much distance you cover. Then, in the morning or whenever you have some time, lay on your back, either on the bed or the floor, put your hands behind the sides of your bottom or, if it is easier for you, behind your legs from the outside just above the fold of your knees, and cycle with your legs in the air. Slowly increase the time you do it until your heart-rate (pulse) is at least 10 -20 more than when you started. This is the minimum. If you want to know your target heart rate you can google it, but then you will probably have to do more strenuous exercises.

A quick way to count your pulse rate is to count it for 6 seconds and then multiply by 10. This is a great exercise for your six pack as well! Of course, if you prefer you can do the full 'bicycle-crunch' exercise. As always be careful if you have a medical condition that may not allow this.

After I have done this I stand up and try to bend down to touch my toes as far as possible 10 times, then squat and rise 10 times, even if have to help myself up by holding on to something. Then I swing my arms out horizontally, first bent at the elbow and then straight 10 times, and lastly, I move my neck in all directions a few times, which you should not do if you experience neck pain. All this only takes a few minutes. I don't say it is as good as going to the gym but this is a good start for people not exercising.

I experienced the value of these exercises when I was a medical student and very busy at that. I did them daily but I suppose three times a week will be enough, or not to do them all on the same day. I once went mountain hiking with other students and when they all complained about painful muscles the next day, I felt fine. The same happened after playing a random friendly rugby match.

Thus, with a set schedule and a disciplined life, you have the power to train your 'inner manager' how to control your life and meet your own and others' expectations. As far as you have control over your thoughts, give priority to positive thoughts, and if they are followed by positive speech and positive actions, with consistency, it will at the end lead to a positive life-style.

Consistent actions based on things you have learned from this book, will over time internalise this knowledge and train your executive functions to support your actions, making it less difficult to adhere to it. Launching into things with determination and enthusiasm can certainly help you overcome the deficiency. I am adding an interesting piece of information which I have copied from appendix 1 at the end of the book "Newer brain research, such as that described by Dr Caroline Leaf in her book: *Who switched off my brain?* **describes how the traditional view that our brains are 'hard wired' is not true. The brain's circuits and even structure can be changed by consistent thought patterns (negative thoughts bring about a decline or shrinking of the nerve cells in our brains, and consistent positive thoughts bring growth and new nerve connections). It could be that some people who have 'outgrown' their ADHD are the ones who have unknowingly applied this principle consistently! "**

In some cases, however, this may still not be enough and you may need to get medication from the doctor. Don't see this as a crutch or an excuse to give up on the other things. Think of it as a part of the toolkit that will keep your life in order (clearing the obstructions). It helps your conscious and subconscious executive functions to become more congruent.

Key Strategies

- Train your inner manager
- Adjust, balance and plan
- Maintain regular physical exercise, a healthy diet and enough sleep
- Ensure optimum use of healthy stimuli

Knowing my limits

Another important strategy that has been helping me control my life has been the knowledge of my limitations. Knowing your limitations is a sign of wisdom not weakness. {17}

You have to realise that you are not always the best person to manage certain areas of your life. For instance, if I had let my wife manage our finances, or at least been more open with her about them, we would have been in a much better financial position than we are now. Delegate or share responsibility for the things you are not so good at to a partner, a trusted friend or a professional service. This is the way to compensate for what you are not able to do best yourself or do not have enough time available to do. If you cannot bring yourself to delegate, it is better to let go of the project than to waste your time and money. {58}

Key Strategies

- Know your limitations
- Be open and seek help
- Delegate and outsource
- Work towards overcoming your limitations

Planning and Organising

There are two forces in the world: chaos on one side, and order on the other side. Anything left on its own without the application of order will eventually deteriorate into chaos. A piece of iron lying outside will rust, and anything organic will decompose.

Take a car, for instance. If you just drive it without getting maintenance done, things will start to go wrong. Eventually it won't run properly and it will stand outside and, as time goes on, it will just become the carcass of a car. Exactly the same principle applies to our minds and bodies. If we don't apply order to them, they start to deteriorate and stop functioning. Because the deterioration may stretch over a long period of time we can deceive ourselves that it won't come, but it will come, like a bad tooth if you don't regularly attend to your teeth.

Fortunately, you can overcome this by getting organised and developing a goal-oriented master plan and a master schedule. Here are a few tactics that I applied to my life and experienced positive results over the years. If you follow these, I can assure you that you will become more organised and your life will feel more fulfilled.

It may sound like extra work, but it will save you hours wasted on looking for things. Most importantly, it will give you the feeling of being in control. One thing I learned from my stepmother which she learned from her mother is that there must be:

A place for everything and everything in its place

Even if you learn and practice nothing else from reading this book, this habit will bring you a change for the better. First find or make a place for everything, and get rid of or store things for which there is no place. Then keep things in their place. This is of critical importance. You mustn't waste time looking for things you need. They must be in place. For instance, know where to find the telephone number of the plumber to call if the toilet is blocked.

As recently as this morning (17/8/17) I learned a lesson for not sticking to this habit. I just could not find the bunch of keys including my car keys and the key to the outside door of the block of flats where we live. I looked everywhere and then I started to think that the only place left to look was in the outside door. Tjey weren't there, but then I saw someone had put them on top of the post boxes in the foyer. This was one of my ADHD errors, though I think it could happen to anybody. I had been distracted by the dog I took for a walk and who didn't want to come in. That is no excuse – I jeopardized the security of myself and others and my car could easily have been stolen. If I had gone to put the keys in their place, I would have noticed immediately that I did not have them. Always putting the keys away as soon as I come in is a safety measure, a bit like a doctor writing a prescription making a mistake and the pharmacist picking it up.

If you walk from one room in the house to another:

Never walk empty handed.

Always carry something that belongs to the other room, like a glass or a cup in at least one of your hands, and inspire the others in your household to do the same. If you come in from your car, bring something to put in the rubbish bin. If you are taking your hands from one place to another anyway, why not put something in them that isn't in its place?

Make it a rule to put away everything you use and clean up afterwards. The idea is not for this to be a burden or an obsession, but an organised way of life.

Soon, you will realise that everyday stress is reducing due to this simple habit!

Be prepared for emergencies

Keep emergency numbers close-by where they can be easily found, especially when you aren't at home. Include the telephone numbers of the ambulance, fire brigade and the police, along with your GP, local hospital, and dentist.

Alongside these, keep the numbers to dial in case of problems with essential utilities, such as electricity, gas and water (including the number to report any gas leaks). Know whom to call if there are problems with electrical appliances or with the plumbing. Keep a back-up copy of all key numbers on your mobile.

I also have particulars in this file to help my loved ones if I should pass away, including particulars of funeral insurance and arrangements and my Will.

Keep the number for a breakdown service for your car at hand, along with your insurance company details. *Get a spare key made today if you don't have one! I have learned a challenging lesson about this when I lost our car keys on the beach!*

Be selective and get your priorities right

Decide which things are important to you and give more attention to them. This way, you will have more time to do these things, because you will not be wasting time on unimportant stuff.

A solution for not overspending time on some things, or leaving them half done, is to have a maximum time for certain activities, whether they are priorities or just things you enjoy. This can apply to watching TV, spending time on Facebook or similar. Be disciplined with this and you will feel more in control of your life. Sometimes you will have to make changes according to circumstances, so be flexible, but have a default schedule to go back to. And remember to respect other people's planned times as well.

In general, it is good practice to apply Pareto's 80/20 rule: *Do the 20% of activities that bring 80% of the results (or at least those that will bring you 80% of the grief if you don't do them!).*

There are certain jobs that will seem to keep you busy forever, and may take up all your time every day. You must take some time off from these responsibilities to do things that are more pressing and important. Once these are done, you can return to the ongoing tasks.

Sometimes I had lots to do but could not figure out where to start, so I spent a lot of time just trying to understand the flow of things. This is not to say you shouldn't make time to relax, but just sitting around doing nothing is entirely different. I used to end up wasting a lot of time and struggling hard to find more time to do all those things that could have been done earlier. All this made me realise the importance of prioritising tasks.

It is better to do the things you don't like to do first. For instance, you like working in the garden but you have to clean the kitchen or the garage. It is better while you are cleaning the kitchen to look forward working in the garden, than to be working in the garden thinking about the mess in the kitchen that needs cleaning. I agree that sometimes you need to do the nice thing first to get strength to do the not so nice one!

Use power tools whenever possible. For instance, use an electric drill or a saw to make your work easier, instead of struggling with tools that take up more of your time. This also applies to getting others involved who may be able to do things better or much quicker than you can, releasing you to spend your time on what you can do best.

Filing and Organising

For this **Master Plan**, you can use any file or case into which you can put dividers with headings. Try to get rid of things that are no longer important/necessary when you put new ones in.

If you move around, have a 'transit file' or 'action file' that you take with you when you leave home; a particular folder in your briefcase, say, or in the bag you always take to work. This is for important things that need to be done that day. Remember to look at it when you get to work and when you get home. Even if you work at home, getting into the habit of using an action file can make life easier. If you have an existing filing system that you're happy with, keep it and keep using it. If your files become congested, try taking out a couple of sheets of paper that are no longer in use for each one you add. Then you won't need to buy another file for a long time.

Make sure that you have a separate file for your goals and projects. This is a very special file, the contents of which should be revised regularly and with excitement! This will enhance your motivation to accomplish tasks. Remember that it mustn't be dormant. Transfer the actions that need to be carried out into your diary. See this area as a very important component of your inner manager. These goals should bring direction to your life. If you do not have your own goals, others will fill your time with their goals.

In your Goals and Projects file, enter a few of the following (not too many) and write them down as: short-term (weeks or months); intermediate (years); and long-term (more than 5 years) projects. For instance: getting the garden/house in order (short-term); planning and saving for a holiday or a study project (intermediate); planning and saving for a bigger home or retirement (long-term). There may be many others, depending on your circumstances.

My diary... My PA

A diary, either a book or electronic, is necessary, but you have to put appointments and tasks into it, look at it regularly, and don't forget the deadlines.
ENTER APPOINMENTS AND IMPORTANT DATES IN YOUR DIARY IMMEDIATELY and also arrange ASAP for whatever arrangements you have to make to attend an appointment.

More Daily Organising...

Collect a library, which may just be a few valuable books to be read regularly to help you achieve your goals. Make a photo library for your memories. Remember, a picture speaks a thousand words.

The experience of how good it feels to know where everything is, and that you are not disorganised and falling behind in doing things on time will be your reward. Also remember that no one is perfect, but you are taking steps in the right direction. This knowledge alone makes it a satisfying undertaking.

You may already have many of the things I've mentioned in place, or you may have an existing system that works well for you. That's fine. If not, don't be discouraged. Take one step at a time, and though it may take a while for you to become organised, you will get there if you persist. Hopefully you will become much more organised than you are now!

Are you like me, inclined just to read the first few lines of instructions or otherwise and then assume the rest? This has brought me into trouble more than once! For instance, someone gives me directions and I get a map of my own in my mind and then get lost. Reading the directions first when you put something together will save you from having to go back a step or two.

Last, but not least, have a notebook near your telephone and regular work place. Never write messages or telephone numbers on loose pieces of paper.

Below is an example of a **Master Plan** that I use for managing the important aspects of my life. You could customize this to create your own Master Plan that will help you organise your letters and documents, and minimise searching time when you need them. Spend some time on this now – it will help you to identify the key problems in your daily life as well.

Example of how to organise your Master Plan.
It may look daunting, but it covers most items, you can use as little or as much of it as you want. For instance, if you do not have that many documents, you may just put your financial stuff under Personal Finances and leave the subdivisions.

A. Emergencies *Telephone numbers and vital documents should be easily located in your filing system*
B. Personal Finances 1. *Bank account* 2. *Credit/debit cards* 3. *Personal loans* 4. *Budget* 5. *Savings* 6. *Mortgage*
C. Insurance 1. *Life* 2. *Other* 3. *Last Will and Testament*
D. Vehicle 1. Servicing and MOT 2. License 3. Registration.
E. Phones 1. *Mobile* 2. *TV* 3. *Computer*
F. Home and Garden 1. *Maintenance* 2. *Groceries and cleaning.* 3. *Gas and electricity* 4. *Registration and other documents*
G. Children 1. *Education* 2. *Activities and other*
H. Health
I. Recreation
J. Personal Growth
K. Family and Friendships
L. My Most Significant Relationship
M. Citizenship

Any of these may need a separate file

Apart from a **Masterplan** to classify your stuff, you should have a **Master Schedule** to ensure that you spend your time wisely and give attention to the right things at the right time. This is an extension of your calendar. **In your Master Schedule include** *protected times* every day which are applicable to home and work situations. Fit it in with the usual activities, it can be for 30 minutes, or any period you can protect on a particular day, but don't skip.

For example:
Monday – *Method*; Planning
Tuesday – *Tasks*; Project management
Wednesday – *Well done!* Finish the unfinished
Thursday – *Tuition*; Study (work-related or other)
Friday – *Find*; Admin
Saturday – *Shine*; Clean; Relax
Sunday – *Steady*; Relationship-building; Forget about work

For instance, I like writing and can do it all day, but on Monday I have to spend some protected time on planning for the week. First, I have a look at my diary and see if my arrangements for appointments and visitors are in place. I also pencil-in protected times for the other days of the week. I look at the week's groceries and medicines and quite a few other things. This takes me the better part of an hour, including interruptions and a cup of coffee, but then I can continue with the rest of my activities for the day.

Or I may have lots of things to do, but on a Tuesday I have to spend some protected time on my projects. In my case, writing and publishing my books. I may use most of a Tuesday for that!

On a Wednesday, you have to spend some protected time on things that are a challenge to you. For instance, your office or kitchen is in a mess. Tackle it! Also, if there is a project that has been outstanding for a long time, work on it. Or perhaps there is a picture that has been sitting there to be framed since long ago, take it to the framing shop. On one Wednesday, I decided to put arranging for a new mobile phone on my protected list, as my contract had run out a month before and instead of taking time for a new contract and a new phone, I just kept on struggling with the old one. But on this Wednesday, I took action and the next day I had my new phone! One thing to ponder is that action breeds action and, if you do not act, those depending on your action won't act either – as happened with the phone. Your action or lack of action can, of course, breed reaction, as when you trespass on someone's property or neglect to pay your bills.

Completion of outstanding issues is so important that you could spend all the time you have on a Wednesday finishing them all. But don't despair, even if you can do only one thing that has been outstanding, you have at least used some of your Wednesday protected time productively. Yesterday was Wednesday and I sold something that I listed the previous Wednesday on eBay. It has been sitting here for many months but now it's done!

Now today is Thursday and I have to practise what I teach. So, though I have many things to do, I have decided to find an article about '*word-finding problems*' and take about an hour to read it thoroughly. To find the correct words when speaking is an intricate process, utilizing and enormous amount of connections in the brain. Also to be able to speak a language, you also need an enormous amount of neurone connections. Of course, Thursdays are not the only day that I read, but on a Thursday, some reading time is protected. If we just go on working without new knowledge, our edge becomes blunt. Studying not only adds to your knowledge but makes you think, especially if you read broader than just your own interest. For instance, on another Thursday, apart from all the other things I have to do I decided to enrol for a short course on *severe asthma* – maybe because my second brother died during an attack of severe asthma. Like ADHD, Asthma is an on-going condition with its implications on quality of life. And what is more, for the time spent and answering the questions correctly, I got a certificate!

On yet another Thursday (I will probably tell you about Thursdays until I finish the book!) I read about **perseveration,** a very interesting subject. It means repeating actions or words and keeping on doing this out of situational or social context. There are different degrees of perseveration, it may just be that someone can't switch properly from one activity to another. This may make you feel that you haven't completed a task when you start with the next one and it feels as if this is holding you back. It may seem as if you just can't develop proper momentum. One type we all suffer from, from time to time, is when a tune is 'stuck' in your head. It may help to replace it with another tune or shout it out loud if possible. The same with other forms of perseveration, try to override it with something else, the perseveration will not necessarily accompany that something else. Hyperfocus on one activity may cause or be associated with perseveration.

First thing one Thursday, I spent about an hour reading an article about metabolic syndrome in *Medscape*. It is a preventable condition, related to being overweight and the development of decreased sensitivity to insulin, and I want my readers to be aware of it. Diabetes type two is usually associated with it, as well as increased fat levels in the blood and fat deposits in places like the liver, which may eventually lead to non-alcoholic liver cirrhosis, a life-threatening condition. Also to hypertension and all its complications. Just as the diagnosis of ADHD depends on the presence of a certain number of symptoms, like restlessness, inattention, inability to finish tasks, and inability to give attention to detail, to name a few, so too with the metabolic syndrome. Apart from the ones I have mentioned a waistline of more than 102 cm (40 inches) in men and 88 cm (35 inches) in women is a wakeup call to do something about it. If this is you, there are not many things more important in your life than to make a serious effort to normalize your weight! A healthy lifestyle helps the production of neurotransmitters. If you are overweight, your lifestyle is not healthy. My book called *Budget Calories - buy your food with Calories*, available from Amazon, has some practical suggestions to help you to attain a normal BMI, but of cause, there are many other resources available to help you. You can easily find out what your BMI is; there are apps on Google .
Another worthwhile health investment is to look well after your teeth, make it part of saving for your retirement! Or even for earlier.

On Fridays, I have to give *Admin* some protected or priority time. This will include looking at my bank accounts and paying outstanding bills, writing letters, and making sure my filing is up to date. I also look at my emergency file and update some of the particulars. I take about an hour for this. For the rest of the day I will be busy with other activities. It is a good habit not to have any unanswered letters or unfiled papers staring at you at the end of Friday,

You still have to have your usual program for the week as well, things that you have to do every day or when they come up. Like cooking, if you are the cook at home. Or putting out the rubbish, if you can't find somebody else to do it!

You can have your protected time at any time during the day that suits you, the earlier, the better though. Don't go to sleep that night before you used some of the protected time! Off course this is the schedule that works for me, you may want to adapt it, just use some of it or make your own. The advantage of having a schedule like this is that it will be unlikely that any of your activities will be left hanging for weeks on end, while you use all your time for routine activities, which may not add to the accomplishment of your goals.

You must also have a way of being reminded of deadlines to finish things. For instance, you can pay a traffic ticket at a discount for a certain number of days, but if you allow the deadline to pass, you will have to pay the full amount. Or if there is a deadline to register for the college and you let it pass you may lose your place. The problem of not doing things before the time expires is that you can't turn back the clock! Go for the motto:

A Time for everything and everything on time

If you do things at the right time, it helps your systems to run smoothly. If you don't adhere to time plans and schedules you will never have the experience of being in control of your life. Systems don't run by themselves, they are dependent on you doing certain things on time. If you don't dedicate the time to do something, the chances are that it won't be done, or at least not as regularly as it should be. Some things you have to do, others you have to make sure that other people do.

For instance, to keep your car on the road, you not only have to put petrol or diesel in and check the oil regularly, but you also have to take it for a service, get an MOT, and pay the insurance and tax on time. If you hear a knock in the engine, it's more likely to get worse rather than go away, unless you do something about it.
If you have to decide between two things to do, ask: "Is this thing going to help my systems run smoothly or is it going to put a spanner in the works?" For things to run smoothly, you need to turn up for appointments on time, pay bills on time, make phone calls on time, water the plants in the garden on time, pay taxes on time, plan your holiday on time, and so on.

Make notes of deadlines in your diary. For example, note down payments you have to make, and create a time for paying them in your daily schedule. Don't allow them to pass by without being done, even if you have to sacrifice one of your other activities. Have an alarm system on your mobile phone to remind you before the deadline passes.

Better still, try to do important things, like paying bills, in advance. Don't go from tackling one crisis to another. Ask for help if you need it. When deadlines pass, you may think they have gone away but they usually come back with a vengeance! The old saying, "*A stitch in time saves nine,*" is still very true. So take a few minutes at the beginning of the day to plan it out. This will save you hours of hard work on less important things. You may also take some time to plan the week, the month and the year. Schedule some time to make your plans. If it can't be done at home, go to work a little earlier and do it there. If you have time to spare, don't wait for it to pass or become bored, fill the void with activity and see how quickly the time passes, and the less there are things left for you to be done.

Below, you'll find a checklist that I prepared based on my experience and have adjusted over the years. As you read it, think how the points fit in with your own life.

Either at the beginning, during the process, or before you carry out a task, come to a definite decision to do it, and see yourself accomplishing it.

Getting-Organised Checklist

On the right side award yourself a 1 (if not yet the best you can be) or a 2 (your best) and check regularly to see which 1s have become 2s. Write N/A if not applicable for you.

A place for everything and everything in its place.	
No walking empty-handed.	
A notebook for messages and phone numbers.	
Get and fill in a main diary and calendar.	
Get and fill in a portable diary.	
Schedule time for leisure activities.	
Be ready for emergencies.	
List everything still to be done. Eliminate one by one.	
Prioritise P1, P2… NP1, NP2… L1, L2…	
Have your master plan and filing system ready.	
Get your action/transit file up and running.	
Use power tools and get help do the job better and/or quicker.	
Use a journal.	
Read books to help you achieve your goals.	
Make a photo library – your memories.	
For each hour you work, spend at least five minutes reading and organising not necessarily the same day.	
Make time for regular, important tasks, e.g. watering, cleaning, washing, cooking etc.	
No waiting for time to pass; fill it with some activity.	

The shorter version is:

Time management.	
Place or space management.	
Resources management.	

Overcoming Poor Concentration

Poor concentration was one of the main things that motivated me to start fighting my attention deficit disorder. I was really disturbed by my lack of concentration during my late twenties. At times, it was the poor quality of concentration – I could recognise that I was unable to get into the depth of things I was reading or doing.

Under some or most circumstances, your ability to concentrate on any one thing for a length of time may be poor. There will be exceptions, such as when you are very interested or excited about something, but in general this may not be the case. The quality of your concentration may also affect your memory; for instance, if you go to do something, and then something else gets your attention along the way, you may forget what you wanted to do in the first place. You can imagine how dangerous this can be when driving, even if you just take a little longer to switch back after your attention was caught by something beside the road. We can also have inner distractions. If you are anxious or depressed, it is difficult to concentrate, but also memories or things you look forward to, picturing them in your mind, can distract you from what you are doing. This has to do with your executive functions.

You will have to make a quality decision to concentrate. Try to remove as many distractions as possible and just keep the essentials. Some people concentrate better with soft music in the background which has a calming effect. Give yourself a time limit, to work under pressure. 'Looping back' your attention means making an effort to keep in contact with your initial activity. If your mind wanders off onto something else, it shouldn't become a separate circle, but just a 'loop'. This habit, which you can teach yourself, may involve going back to the original point where you were distracted. Always ask yourself, "What did I come here for in the first place?" and do that first.

Try and concentrate on one thing at a time. You should also keep in mind what you are going to do next, so you don't waste time between activities and interrupt your flow of concentration. Always have another activity 'up your sleeve', then if you get stuck with the first one for a while you won't waste time while waiting.

Don't have too many things on your table when you work, ideally only those necessary to carry out the task at hand. Try to work with as few external distractions as possible, e.g. check emails only at certain times, and don't allow other people's urgencies to interrupt you if you are in the position to do so. (You might have to be careful how you communicate this to your boss!)

In summary then, you are where your attention is. This is why it is so dangerous when you use your mobile phone when driving when you and your attention are with the person you are talking to there will be moments when your car is effectively without a driver! You must consistently be on your alert for distractions.

Eliminate and CONCENTRATE

Key Strategies

- Try to concentrate on one thing at a time
- Try to minimise clutter on your work table
- Avoid checking emails and other messages too often
- Keep the next task in mind but don't dwell on it before finishing the task at hand

Overcoming poor concentration checklist

On the right-side award, yourself a 1 (not yet the best you can be) or a 2 (your best) and check regularly to see which 1s have become 2s.
Write N/A if not applicable to you.

Create chunks of time for finishing important tasks.	
Follow a specific program and a steady flow of activities.	
Keep just the papers you need for the current task on your desk.	
Eliminate external and internal distractions as far as possible.	
Follow a healthy exercise, eating and sleeping plan.	
Reward yourself for completed tasks. Don't work all the time.	
Concentrate on one task at a time and do it properly.	
Always have another task in mind to carry on with if you get temporarily stuck or finish the first one.	
Get everything ready before you start anything.	

Developing Memory Power

Forgetfulness may be one of the signs of ADHD, but there are many people who don't suffer from ADHD and yet forget things just as easily. This may be one of the most annoying problems and is usually not understood by those with a good memory. It may bring criticism from others, and resentment towards them from you. Don't allow this to happen. *There are positive steps you can take to overcome this!*

You may try memory-training exercises, which are freely available online. The problem is remembering to apply them! Don't let it get you down.

Here are a few simple steps that I followed to support my memory. I use a reminder system, writing the things I want to remember in my diary. You could also make a To Do list on your mobile phone, if that is more convenient to you.

(A note from the Editor. Don't scribble things in a made-up shorthand assuming you will understand them later – take a few extra seconds to write them down in full. Many times I have been left staring at a 'reminder' wondering "what on earth did I mean by that?"!)

I use a pocket-sized diary with a small inside pouch on the front and back covers in which I slip my credit card and driver's licence and I always keep it with me. (You may of course carry these in your wallet.) Make a practice of looking regularly at your diary.

You could use your memory for everyday activities, but I would suggest not relying on it for important appointments and things that have to be done.

Another important practice that will help you live effectively even with a poor memory is to ensure that you put everything in the right place as soon as you get home or get to work. If you visit somewhere and you are wearing a coat which you will take off, put your car keys in your coat pocket, so you won't drive off without your coat. Have other things to act as reminders, like in the old times a knot in your handkerchief.

Get into the habit of doing certain activities at a regular time; watering the plants in the lounge on Sundays, for example. Creating simple habits like these will help you to remember. You may find it worthwhile to do first the things you are most likely forget. When you have to make a note of some things, write down the part that you are most likely to forget first. For instance if something happened at a certain date, write the date first and then the rest.

Here are a few other tactics that have helped me live effectively with a poor memory:

- When you walk, take a keen interest in the things around you. Even make a note of some, and see how many you can remember later. Make it a habit each time you go for a walk. This exercises your 'memory brain.'
- Associate people's names and faces with others you already know, or with other characteristics.

- Create funny and strange mental images to make remembering easy and fun. For instance, if you have to buy chicken at the supermarket, think of a chicken running away chased by a famer with a big knife! You won't forget that easily.
- Try to relax by taking deep breaths (not hyperventilating!) and relax the muscles you don't actively use at that point – you will concentrate and remember better.
- Associations help you remember:

One – sun

Two – glue

Three – tree

Four – door

Five – dive

Six – mix

Seven – heaven

Eight – gate

Nine – line

Ten - den

Don't you think you will impress people and yourself if you can name ten items in order or, for instance, say which one was number seven immediately? Well with this method you can.

For instance – you have 10 food and other items to buy at a shop: Make a picture of 1. Margarine all melted in the sun 2. An apple glued to a table and someone trying to get it loose. 3. A chicken getting into a tree when the farmer chases it. 4. Someone falling over cold drinks as he enters a door, and so on – make a list of things and try it.

You can also think about certain items in certain rooms of a house and you can remember even more if you attach a few items to one you are remembering. For instance, fruit and then different fruit attached to one another or a cow, and then think of meat, milk, butter. It may be easier just to make a list, but it will be less fun!

Developing Memory Power Checklist

On the right-side award, yourself a 1 (not yet the best you can be) or a 2 (your best) and check regularly to see which 1s have become 2s.

Write N/A if not applicable to you.

Taking interest in your environment.	
Associating people's names and faces.	
Create funny and strange mental pictures.	
Use these mental pictures associated with words rhyming with numbers.	
Relaxing.	
Always put keys, diary etc. in the same place.	
Make use of your mobile phone or other device for reminders.	
Get into the habit of doing things regularly at a certain time.	

Driving with Attention Disorder

Accidents do not happen by accident!
(Dr Tariq Bhatti)

I soon discovered that, because I had attention disorder, I had to work harder to stay concentrated while driving. People with ADHD are up to four times more likely than other drivers to be involved in motor vehicle accidents. I am convinced that this figure can be lowered significantly if one drives responsibly, and take a break when you become tired. An attitude that caused me to drive more carefully is to see driving as a priviledge, not a right because there are many people who are not allowed to drive due to a illness, a disability or other reason.

Sometimes your attention is briefly caught by something beside the road, or in the car. Even if you take just a little longer to switch back, that second or two can mean the difference between good driving and an accident. It has been suggested that people with severe ADHD should only be allowed to drive when they are on medication. This is not law yet, but it's even more reason to be extra careful when driving.

If you tend to get lost when driving, you may need to invest in a satellite navigation system, follow a good map, or have someone travel with you to give you directions. Fortunately, like anything else, once you have followed a route several times, it will become easier to remember. This is what happened to me in Texas, (46) but after I drove to Chris Lyon's house a few more times, I did not get lost anymore.

Here are a few more suggestions for you for safe driving.
- Keep your car and tyres in peak condition, driving slowly and carefully in difficult conditions, whilst also avoiding sudden acceleration, braking and turning, you will stand a better chance of keeping control of your vehicle.
- Try not to do things impulsively, like suddenly turning into a side road without indicating in advance. Be even more careful when driving when you are in a hurry.
- If you don't see a turn until the last minute, go past and find a place to turn around.
- Always try to relax and concentrate on the road ahead.
- Never talk on a mobile phone, or get so absorbed in a conversation (or argument) with your passengers that you forget what is going on around you.
- If you are new driver, it is a good idea to limit the number of passengers for the first year or so.
- Make a habit not to look at things around the road when driving. Let them stay in your peripheral visual area.
- Adjusting the radio or air conditioning while driving at a high speed can cause you to drive off the road in seconds; that is why there is a warning on your sat-nav not to make adjustments while driving.
- Make a habit of putting your seat belt on before you drive off, and not along the way.
- Stay within the speed limit, even if others get impatient – that is their problem, not yours!
- Be even more careful not to drink or take drugs when you drive. The police will take it very seriously if you do something wrong, and your breath smells of alcohol. Being

caught under the influence when behind the wheel can mean a ban from driving, a fine of up to £5000, a criminal record and potentially community service. If a fatality is caused by drink driving, then a mandatory prison sentence will follow. Whilst there is a legal limit for alcohol intake when driving (35mg alcohol per 100ml of breath), its effects on the body differ from person to person. Factors such as height, weight and gender can affect its impact, meaning that even small amounts of alcohol can be too much for some people. ADHD is a complicating factor too. The safest thing is simply, don't risk it.

Key Strategies
- Concentrate on the road ahead and try to avoid any distractions
- Never talk on a mobile phone
- Minimise intense conversation with passengers

Driving with ADHD Checklist

On the right-side award, yourself a 1 (not yet the best you can be) or a 2 (your best) and check regularly to see which 1s have become 2s.

Write N/A if not applicable to you.

Do not do things on impulsive.	
If you miss a turning, go past and find a place to turn around.	
Relax and concentrate.	
Do not use a mobile phone	
New drivers – limit the number of passengers.	
Do not stare at things beside road.	
Do not adjust the sat nav, air con, or radio while driving.	
Put your seatbelt on before driving off.	
Obey speed limits.	
Never drink and drive.	

Suicide

Because it is an important 'side effect' of ADHD I have included this short chapter on a subject I also mentioned it in part one. According to some studies, the suicide rate amongst teens and adults is about five times higher in the ADHD-affected population than in the non-ADHD population. The obvious reason for this seems to be depression triggered by their failure to meet their own and their family's expectations.

More women have been observed to be affected than men. Girls and women with ADHD are more difficult to diagnose and need more specialised treatment, mainly because of important co-morbidities; depression and sometimes OCD. Psychiatric treatment is indicated for this, and if medication is considered it should target not only the ADHD but also the OCD and depression, which can both be treated with an anti-depressant. Psychologically they need help to improve their self-worth and image, otherwise they tend to try and boost it by indulging in alcohol or other drugs, and unhealthy relationships.

At times, suicide seems to be the only solution to their problems, though most of the time people commit suicide for reasons that could have been resolved. They generally do it on the spur of the moment, having been traumatised by recent experiences. However, these impulses can be mastered with patience and perseverance. I also had such moments long ago when I just felt like ending my life. My faith helped me through those and many other difficult situations and I am grateful for that. As this book contains principles that can be applied by anybody, I am not going to discuss my faith here – that aspect of life I leave to the reader to explore for him or herself. Talking to others also helped me and, as I mentioned earlier, the fact that I have gone through life with ADHD has helped me to develop more resilience in terms of prevailing against the odds.

I have found that the easiest way to conquer an emotional outbreak is to talk to someone and confide in the right person. If you have no idea where to start, you could try your doctor or visit this web site:
http://www.nhs.uk/Conditions/Suicide/Pages/Getting-help.aspx
As someone who has gone through this, I would suggest being open about the problem and ready to share your experiences. If you put up a false image of yourself, you will always be worried that your weakness might be noticed or discovered. This creates more stress and aggravates the problem. The best way is to face the truth and be transparent, while continuously organising and changing your lifestyle to resolve the issues. To be honest, I am also still working hard to stop hiding my weaknesses and portray the true 'me'!

Motor Coordination

A number of people with symptoms of ADHD have problems with coordination. This can be a real problem at work or other places, where you may be embarrassed by your clumsiness. Try to avoid difficult situations wherever possible, and try to laugh at yourself rather than feel humiliated.

The control of movement is very complex and on three levels, the cerebral cortex, the brainstem regions and the spinal cord which extends into the limbs and other organs of movement. The mechanics of how muscles, bones and joints come to purposeful movements under the direct control of nerves from the spinal cord, is a miracle of engineering in itself. The cerebellum or small brain plays an important role in the coordination process and, together with the inner ear, in balance. Sensory feedback, especially from the muscles and the skin, is very important. The sensory and motor areas of the brain are in approximation and near to the areas responsible for ADHD and other neurodevelopment problems. The Limbic System is the main seat of emotions and reticular formation in the brain stem controls, amongst other things, sleep, arousal and attention.

Poor motor coordination has an effect on your ability to write, play sport and conduct your everyday life. It also has a detrimental effect on self-image and confidence. Exercises may help a little, but at the end you have to learn how to compensate for it like for any other handicap.

Perception

Looking but not seeing properly, or listening but not hearing properly, sums up problems with perception. In other words someone's eyes and ears may be normal, but the way the impulses register in the brain are distorted. Visual and auditory perception problems frequently accompany ADHD. If someone continually misunderstands words or fails to see somethings that are obvious for others, he or she may need an assessment.

Visual impulses are transferred by neurones from the retina of the eye to the occipital lobe of the brain where we 'see.' Assessment and treatment of visual perception problems is done by an Occupational Therapist.

Auditory impulses are transferred from the cochlea of the inner ear to the upper part of the temporal lobes where we 'hear.' Though not so simple, that is why auditory perception problems falls under the umbrella of Auditory Processing Disorders (APD) Assessment and treatment of these is done by a Speech and Language Therapist

Both visual perception and auditory processing play a role when reading because we associate the written word with how it sounds.

We also perceive with our other senses, like touching, tasting and smelling. All the senses are interrelated, so as to store memories of different situations. For instance, the smell of a certain perfume may make you 'see' someone. Therefore, though there are certain areas in the brain used more specifically for reception of sight and hearing, we really see and hear with our whole brain due to all the connections. If we see or sudden danger coming our way, our whole body jumps into action under control of our brain.

Treatment programs do not always solve the problems, but after having had a formal assessment one may know to give attention to certain issues. Here is an example of how you may go about it after receiving a diagnosis of APD.

Listen more carefully to what people say, even lip reading them. It is difficult not to make people feel you are staring at them but, even so, that may be better than wrongly interpreting what they are saying. It may also be of value to give feedback to the person in some way and make sure what you think you have heard is what he or she meant. For instance, if someone says "Let's meet at twelve o'clock," you might say, "Is twelve o'clock the best time for you?" You can also make notes to go over later, but taking notes while people talk may make them feel uncomfortable, so it may be better to do it just afterwards and call them if you are not sure of something.

The reasons for sight and auditory problems may be unknown, hereditary, environmental, infections and brain damage by birth, accident or a stroke. Anxiety makes them worse. I may have a touch of visual perception problems – sometimes I find myself looking for things that are right in front of me!

Specific Learning Disorders

According to DSM-5 (the standard mental-health classification used by medical professionals) the following diagnostic criteria specify learning disorders:

- Problem(s) with learning and at least the use of one of the academic skills below, even though interventions have been tried.
- Performance in those area(s) substantially below expectation with resulting significant functional impairment.
- Problems began in school age, although may have not become apparent until demands exceed skills.
- Difficulties exceed those expected with any associated environmental, sensory, intellectual or other impairment.

Specific learning disorders:

1. ...with impairment in reading (dyslexia).
2. ...with impairment in written expression. *(formerly known as Dysgraphia)*
3. ...with impairment in mathematics (dyscalculia).

All of these are also classified into mild, moderate, and severe, and there are further subdivisions.

It is beyond the scope of this book to talk about assessment and treatment. These should be done by a professional with the expertise to do so. All I can add is that only reading problems should really bother an adult in this day and age. There are mobile phones for memos and calculations, a camera or scan for documents and a spell check on your computer. If your grammar has to be checked there are editors available – either electronic or in person.

I have typed all my books with two fingers. I suppose I could have dictated them, but I did not always have a private secretary to do the typing for me and I think better when I type. Voice recognition devices are another option, but my accent makes it more difficult, though I suppose I could train it to overcome that problem. Or maybe I should have gone for elocution classes! My only problem with the spell check is when I spell the word so wrong that it can't come up with a correction. Then I go to Google, which asks me if that was what I meant and then gives me what is hopefully the correct word! Anyhow, I knew a Professor in psychiatry who could not spell at all. He passed all his exams orally and his secretary typed all that needed to be written.

Developing and Keeping Momentum

When I was a student, I was working with an ambulance crew in the countryside. One day when we were travelling, the left rear wheel came loose and, as we ground to a halt, I saw the wheel bowling away from the ambulance with one of the male nurses running after it. The wheel had momentum when on the ambulance and when it came loose it kept its momentum for a while. I saw it hit an anthill and jump into the air, and when it landed on the other side it carried on running until eventually it lost its momentum, as it had no driving force of its own.

Through this incident, I found that the secret is for us to cultivate our inner driving force by steady attainment, in order to keep our momentum. That is an important part of our executive function.

The earth spins due to its momentum, and we are travelling with it at a speeds varying from zero at the poles (just rotating) to more than 1000 miles per hour if we are near the equator. Time is ticking away constantly, related to the earth's momentum. If we walk, our momentum is in a forward direction as long as we do not stop or turn sideways.

Definition of momentum: (Encarta World English Dictionary)
1. *Capacity for progressive development*: the power to increase or develop at an ever-growing pace – e.g. "The project was in danger of losing momentum."
2. *Forward movement*: the speed or force of forward movement of an object. The momentum gained on the downhill stretches of the course.

I do not suggest that we must be like a wheel driven by a motor, but that we should have momentum in pursuing our goals. This entails 'spinning quietly' even when we are relaxing, ready for the next action! Having momentum in our actions need not be a teeth-grinding, pressing-forward-at-all-costs experience. We do have to expend energy, but selectively making choices will do just as much to keep us moving in the right direction. Keeping momentum going in our actions is part of a winning strategy with optimum use of energy.

Now this is easier said than done, especially for the person with executive function problems, but there are ways to tackle it:

Make quality decisions about what you want for your life and write them down in detail in your journal. Keep looking at them and make additions and adjustments as time goes on. (This should be your 'life's momentum') Be excited about it and don't be put off from pursuing it by anyone or anything. Get help if you feel you can't do it alone.

Your Quality decisions need to be informed decisions. If you make decisions, the contributing factors will never be a hundred percent on the one side and zero on the other, you must decide which side weighs the heaviest, and choose that one. Almost like a democratic election! The most stress is caused when you get caught up in the middle of two possible decisions, or if you bounce backwards and forwards between two options. Remember that you must have had a good reason to have made the decision in the first place, and if the reason is still valid, stick with it, even if your feelings about it have changed. You should guard against your decisions and promises being 'situational,' in that as soon as you leave one situation and go to another you forget why you decided on a course of action or promised to do something previously and just don't keep to your decision. Write down in a few words why you made an important decision, so it is not a case of 'out of sight, out of mind.'

This advice is not meant for you to become rigid, but to keep your momentum going steadily. Two things that can really interfere with your momentum are procrastination and absent-mindedness, meaning that your mind is not in the same place as you are. This is usually due to an internal distraction of your thoughts and may also lead to accidents in the same way as talking on a mobile phone and becoming oblivious to your surroundings.

1. Plan your day and try to adhere to the plan, but don't get frustrated about obstacles or interruptions, see them as unavoidable but temporary things to overcome; keep your momentum going. Live above the circumstances and not under them. If things get very difficult, just say to yourself: "I will just be the best me I can be." Don't give up, but be prepared to make adjustments when changes seem necessary. If you don't have much to do on a specific day, make sure you do something, even if it is just one small thing. The planning, the doing and thinking about it afterwards, is enough to get you out of bed!

2. Concentrate on one thing at a time but have the next in mind so you do not have to waste time between tasks thinking what to do next.

3. Motivation and goal-setting are key factors in keeping momentum. You also have to make the right choices, linked together with discipline, commitment, attitude, fitness (both physically and mentally), integrity and allocating time for important tasks or projects. Without these your project will not move forward. (See the chapter on organising; it will help you to stay in control.) Ask yourself if at the very moment, "Am I doing the best thing I can do?" Here is a simple mathematical formula, 'The Best Me Formula for Success', to help you:

KNOWLEDGE/PLANNING (2) x RESOURCES (2) x ENOUGH TIME (2) x ATTITUDE/RELATIONSHIPS (2) x EFFORT (2) x CONSISTENCY (2) = RESULT (64)

If you apply your best to each item – the best you can do, not the best compared with others – award yourself a 2. If not, you get 1.

Compare the following and see how it affects your results if you substitute a 1 for a 2

$$2 \times 2 \times 2 \times 2 \times 2 \times 2 = 64$$

$$2 \times 2 \times 1 \times 2 \times 2 \times 2 = 32$$

$$2 \times 1 \times 2 \times 1 \times 2 \times 2 = 16$$

$$1 \times 1 \times 1 \times 1 \times 1 \times 1 = 1$$

HOW FAST DO YOU WANT YOUR WHEEL TO SPIN?

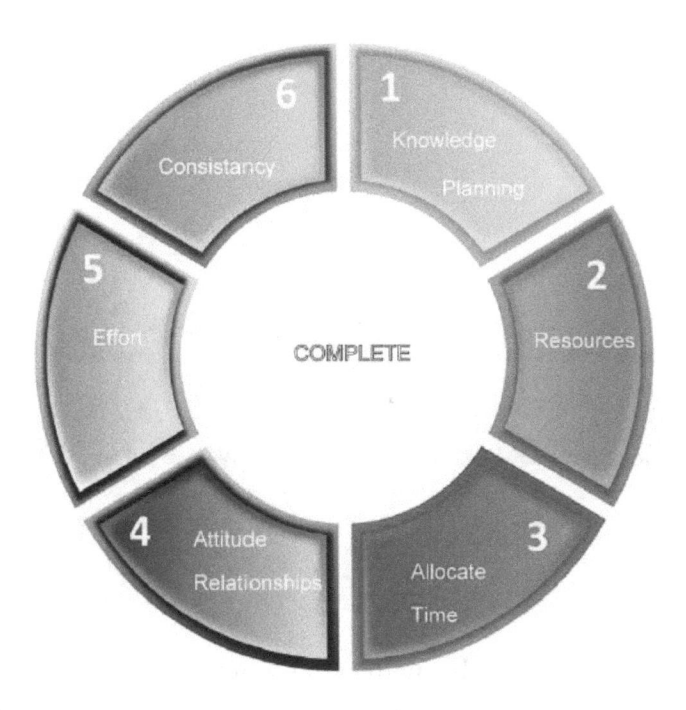

Remember the elements of the formula by looking at the people in the picture below. When you go on a bike trip: (1) you have to plan the trip and everything that goes with it; (2) you have to provide the appropriate resources (bike, food, water); (3) you have to schedule enough time for it; (4) you have to be enthusiastic and have the right attitude, including towards your companions; (5) you have to put the required effort in; (6) you have to pedal consistently!

However, if you fight with your companions, your bike is unreliable, you go in the wrong direction and have to turn back, you do not put in enough effort (especially uphill) and stop frequently, others will reach the destination long before you, and you may never arrive.

You can use this formula to start, execute and evaluate the outcome of any task by giving points for the result. Then look at the items on the left side of the equation, decide on which of them you are losing points and try to improve on these. It is said that the greatest enemy of the best is not the worst, but the second best. So after finishing, a chunk of a task, simply give yourself 1 or 2 for each of the items in the formula. (2 if you executed it the best you were able to or 1 if it was your second best.) You will be surprised how your final marks (results) are reduced when you substitute only one of the twos with a one. You will also see immediately where you need to be more careful the next time.

Always reduce the size of any task by taking away visible chunks. For example: If the kitchen is in a mess, first put away or discard everything that doesn't need to be on the worktops. Then tackle the dishwasher if you have one, afterwards wash the bigger stuff and do a final clean up. With each chunk that is removed the task will look less daunting and this will surely add to your momentum. Even if you are called away at some stage, you will know exactly where to recommence. Apply this strategy to any sizable task you have to do.

If you have a problem being on time for meetings or getting things done in time, try the following: Plan the steps you have to follow 'backwards.' For instance, if you need to attend a meeting at a specific place at 10 am and you have to go by train, you may estimate that the venue is a 20-minute walk from the station, so you will have to arrive there no later than 9.40. If the train journey takes 30 minutes, you need to be on the train as near to 9 o'clock as the timetable allows. If it takes you 15 minutes to get from your home to the station, add on another 15 minutes for parking and buying a ticket, and don't leave your home any later than 8.30 am.

Another example might be that you have to finish a writing project at a certain time (19th November). Start by estimating how long it will take to edit your final draft (7 working days – 10th November), how long it will take you to write the draft (14 days – 25th October), how much time you need to gather information about it (14 days – 11th October), how long to write down the details of the project (2 or 3 days – 7th October), so the project must be started in the first week of October. You don't have to be rigid, but see the different dates as deadlines. There are simpler and quicker ways to plan, but this one will work for anyone who needs a strategy.

Momentum – keeping going – is dependent on discipline rather than feelings, though feelings may affect it. The speed that you walk, for instance, may be affected by your mood but, even so, if you keep putting one foot in front of the other, you will still cover the distance. The good news is that once you begin to act, feelings generally take a back seat and can be kept there until the job is done. Have you ever noticed how fast a feeling can change once you take the lead? Part of maturing emotionally is being able to let your feelings know who is in charge. And, because you have accomplished something and didn't give in to your feelings, you are likely to feel much better.

This is not to say that you must live your life by some rigid framework; a healthy self-discipline allows for some flexibility – but not an excessive amount. The two greatest enemies of keeping a steady momentum are distraction and procrastination, (sometimes a little push may help!) {66}) both of which drag you down. You now know how to deal with these 'enemies'. Go through the checklist to see how to improve your momentum, an important aspect of your life.

Developing-and-maintaining-momentum checklist

On the right-side award, yourself a 1 (not yet the best you can be) or a 2 (your best) and check regularly to see which 1s have become 2s.

Write N/A if not applicable to you.

Have both long and short-term goals.	
Plan to reach those goals and keep at it.	
Implement the BestMe Formula for Success.	
Tackle a daunting task chunk by chunk.	
Be on time for meetings and deadlines.	
Control distractions e.g. phone, PC, TV.	
Try to follow a healthy diet and get enough sleep, exercise and recreation.	
Stay on one task until it is finished, even if you work intermittently because of impulsiveness and inconsistency.	
Concentrate on one thing at a time, but try to have the next in mind, so not waste time switching.	
Try not to make sudden decisions – but when you do come to a final decision - go for it!	
If the task is not that interesting, keep your mind on the reward.	
Do first the things that may have important positive or negative consequences.	
Consider putting a reward and penalty system in place.	

Don't be afraid to admit if you've made an incorrect decision due to impulsiveness; put it right if you can or live with it.	
Cultivate a healthy self-discipline so you are not ruled by your feelings.	

If this aspect of your life is a constant struggle, you may want to add these books to your library *(you should really have a library, even if is only a shelf in a cupboard)*:

Delivered from Distraction
By E.M. Hallowell & J.J. Ratley

How to get things done without trying too hard
By R. Templar

Money Management

Here are some lessons I learned by getting very close to the edge of the cliff. I had been earning and spending with very little planning, just paying bills, household spending, and similar as they arose. Due to my ADHD I was rushing through life without realising the money-management blunders that I was committing. I have learnt from my mistakes so I can tell you how to avoid them.

Never spend more than you earn – it is not yours. And the money you have to pay for income tax is not yours either, don't spend it. Unless you have experience with accounting, the easiest way to monitor what happens with your money is to have four columns on graph paper each month with the following headings: Spendable Income; Total Expenses for the Month; Accumulated Income for the Year So Far; Accumulated Expenditure for the Year So Far. The best way to see what is happening with your money is to have a proper budget. I have mine on excel where I list my income in one column, and then my budgeted expenses in another column, and in a column next to that my real expenses as they come up.

Instead of wishing your income were higher, scrutinise your present expenditure. Is there any way you can save on your mortgage, gas, electricity, telephone, groceries, eating out, etc.? Here are some suggestions to help curb overactive spending:
1. As mentioned, have a proper budget and stick to it. 'A place for every pound, and every pound in its place.' If you haven't got a budget, start now before you read any further.

2. Pay and save. Pay every debt and have a definite savings plan for worthwhile things. Keep someone informed about your finances (like a partner or friend), and talk to them before you embark on any significant spending. It is of the utmost importance to contain impulsive spending. Remember that if you buy something new it will be second-hand immediately you've bought it and worth much less than you paid for it.

3. Try to live on 80% of your income from your first payday onwards. Save 10% for the day you retire (If you start when you are young this will grow to a significant amount with interest, and will help you to retire in peace, not in pieces!). Even if you are not so young when you start, it will still help. Give the other 10% to your church or to a good cause or to those less fortunate than you. This is just a suggestion, but most people acknowledge that giving time and money to others in need brings more happiness into their own lives.

(Jim Rohn suggests in one of his presentations that we should actually try to live on 70% of our income and use the third 10% to release our entrepreneur spirit, e.g. by buying something, repairing it and selling it for a profit.) Whatever you do, protect your budget!

4. Use self-discipline. If you sell your home to buy another one, put the profit you make on the first house into the next instead of spending it on something else. Otherwise you will remain at the bottom of the property ladder.

5. Pay your taxes on time.

6. Don't invest money you can't afford to lose, even if you feel enticed by the amount you may be able make. It is not really yours, and when you lose it you end up owing. The principle

of investing wisely is to utilise the resources that are not used. It is like a hybrid car, you invest when going downhill and use your resources to get it uphill.

7. Pay any bill that has to be paid ASAP. You will have one less thing to worry about.

A last word about debt. Debt is something in your life that holds you back. Not having debt is setting you free to move on, and this does not only apply to owing money. *If you make a promise which you do not keep you are 'indebted' to that person.* 'Debt' can arise if you pass the deadline for doing something and you have not done it. If you do not spend sufficient time with your loved ones, you owe them. Procrastination can be the biggest reason for debt. Doing things that have to be done correctly and on time and not using time or money that you do not have will lead to a (debt) free life.

These guidelines will probably not address all of your financial problems, but they will go a fair way towards doing so, and will keep you out of many troubles. If you are already in trouble, get professional help before it goes any further. Don't give up; even if it is sometimes painful, there is always a way out.

Key strategies
- Plan your budget
- Try to live on 80% of your income
- Control impulsive spending

Money-management checklist

On the right side award yourself a 1 (not yet the best you can be) or a 2 (your best) and check regularly to see which 1s have become 2s.

Write N/A if not applicable to you.

Put income and expenditure controls in place (cash flow). HAVE A WORKING BUDGET.	
Do not spend more than you earn.	
Continually scrutinise your expenditure.	
Plan for a better income (e.g. improve your qualifications).	
If you sell property invest again in property.	
Get out of debt – make a repayment plan.	
Save for worthwhile things, rather than losing money by buying cheap or unnecessary ones.	
Make a retirement plan. Save 10% monthly.	
Keep someone trustworthy informed about your financial situation.	
Pay bills on time, including tax.	
Have an emergency fund for unforeseen expenses.	
File all financial documents and correspondence somewhere safe and easy to access.	
Have a place to keep important shopping receipts.	

Whatever you do, do not compromise your values.

Healthy Relationships

This is such an important issue; possibly the number one reason for happiness and unhappiness in this world. (The second being financial problems and mismanagement of income.) I am confident that, if your close relationships are not smooth, life is disturbed.

In short, relationship problems stem from the following:
1. Misunderstanding the feelings and intentions of others.
2. Being dishonest or inconsistent.
3. Doing things without sharing them with those who ought to know (e.g. spending money without telling your partner).
4. Not doing what you said you would do, breaking promises.
5. Poor money management.
6. Anger outbursts.

There is no quick fix for these issues. You just have to learn from experience and observation and, on the way, you will make mistakes. Everybody makes mistakes in their relationships. Never see yourself as a failure, but instead learn from it and try not to make the same mistake again. Before you respond out of anger, try to make sure that you have the correct information. Many times, this may not be the case and then you have to back-track on your words. If you lose you temper, try to 'find it' before you act!

Communicating with others is the essence of life, whether you like it or not. When you are in someone's company, give them your full attention. Look at their face and body language, and listen to what they are saying – to the words and the meaning behind the words.

For some, this may be more difficult, but you will gain experience if you try. Only reply after you have listened well, and don't expect others to know what you want to say if you don't say it. They aren't mind readers!

It is so sad to see a mother pushing a child in a push chair and, instead of interacting with him, talking on her mobile phone all the time. When this same child grows up the mother will blame him for not talking to her. There are a few windows of opportunity along the way, to help a child to become a responsible and happy person. First, is the bonding time starting just after birth. Then developing a good relationship with them, giving attention to the points I mention below. During the teenage years, you must try to be someone he or she will be proud of, if only when they look back later.

At some time, you will maybe have to make a real sacrifice as you put the child's interest first. That may be difficult and inconvenient for you for a few years, but it may shape the rest of the child's life for the good. I suppose there are limits as to what you can do, but one of my patients' mothers told me that her mum travelled eighty-five miles a day by bus for three days a week to look after her children in order to allow her to attend college, for three years. This is an extreme example, but shows you what can be done.
Don't expect children to appreciate your sacrifices, they will do that later when they look back.

When bringing up children, follow these simple guidelines and I can guarantee they will be happier and cause you less trouble.

1. Give the child lots of love and acceptance.

2. Give more quality attention, and less presents.

3. Discipline. A child has its own agenda, if you do not discipline him, he will discipline you.

4. Lead by example and not only with words.

If you still struggle getting your children to obey, you may want to enrol for one of the courses ADDISS offers on Dr Thomas Phelan's training program: 1-2-3 Magic.

Be honest in your dealings with others. Don't say what you don't mean, but on the other hand, don't say things that will hurt or annoy others if it is not absolutely necessary – even if it is true. If it must be said, try not to say it at a time that is embarrassing to the other person. You need friends not enemies. If you have a reason to praise someone, do so, but with honesty and not flattery. Try to get into the habit of not talking about others if they are not there, as this may be construed as gossip. If the conversation turns in this direction, don't participate; it is very easy to be drawn into gossip.

Sometimes it is very difficult to tell the truth, especially if you have been told off many times in the past. But it is always better to tell the truth, and take the flack, rather than to lie about something. The truth has a funny way of coming out in the end, and lies will become even more of an embarrassment to you. They can also get you into big trouble.

Integrity goes with honesty. This means to be true to others and true to yourself at all times. It also means to take responsibility for your own actions, and not to blame others all the time. If you damage someone's car, or even just scratch it slightly, take responsibility. Don't look around to check whether or not someone saw you, and drive away. That's breaking the law.

The same factors apply to relationships. If you 'scratch' someone, apologise and try to make amends for the damage. If the other person is still upset, then let it remain their problem, not yours. The most important step you can take on your road to being a person with integrity is to keep your word (promises) every time. Even if it hurts, in the end it will repay you.

As a child, you may have been told off and rejected frequently and this made you feel angry. The people who are with you now may not know where you come from, and may find it difficult to understand why you become so easily angered, leading to more rejection and unhappiness. Early attachment problems are sometimes over-emphasised, but they are real and affect the person's sensitivity to rejection. In this respect, attachment and rejection may be two sides of the same coin. There is professional help available. Ask your GP to refer you to a psychiatrist or a psychologist. Also think about issues that may have hurt you in the past and discuss them with someone you can trust. Talking with someone helps clarify things in your own mind. Try to leave your past behind you, and to turn over a new page. Don't expect more from others than you expect from yourself, and remember – forgiving brings more healing to you than to the other person.

Keep 'short accounts' of what others do to you. If you have said or done something that affects a relationship, saying that you are truly sorry about it seldom fails to bring healing, even if it may take some time for the other person to forgive you entirely. Do not qualify your apology by telling the other person what he or she did. If necessary, discuss this before you come to the point of apologising. Try to see the good in others and respect them for that, even if it may not be easy.

If you are in a position to help someone, just do it – you will find it greatly rewarding. Do not, however, intrude on other people's personal space. This means not coming too near or being too familiar with people you are not intimate with. This doesn't mean that you shouldn't have warmth and love for others – that is something different. It is a matter of having a healthy respect for yourself, and for others – including what is their property. Have you noticed how much effort we put into borrowing something we need, and how little effort we put into giving it back when we don't need it any longer?

When you go about helping others, it is essential to make sure that they want your help. I don't like it when I am busy trying to figure out something and someone who knows better, or thinks he knows better, comes up with un-asked-for advice – I may still be able to tolerate that – but not instructions, or even worse, a complete take-over what I am trying to do. It comes across as, at best, over-protection and at worst arrogance. I feel like telling that person, "Just give me a break please!"

Try to make people feel they are important to you at all times. If you are in a conversation with someone and an old friend or a business associate turns up, do not just switch your attention and leave the first person in the lurch – this is not good manners. Even if the new person is important to you, take just a moment to greet him or arrange to talk to him after you have 'rounded off' your existing conversation.

Remember, the telephone is not all-important. In order for you to answer it, you have to interrupt anything you are doing – if you are expecting an important call, warn the person you are with that such a call may come through. A colleague once told me how he drove two hundred miles to meet with the principal of his daughter's college. The man's answering of 'important' calls frequently interrupted their conversation. After the fourth time, my colleague asked the man if there was a telephone nearby. "Of course," the man said, "in the next room. Will it be a local call?"

"Yes" came the answer, "I want to call you." The man asked his secretary not to put any more calls through during the rest of the meeting!

Stand firm when everything goes wrong around you, even if you are accused of something – whether you have done it or not. It is always better if you stick to the truth. Don't lash out and try to protect yourself by attacking others. Rather, see how the problem can be solved, and do the best you can in the circumstances. This is not to say you should allow others to walk all over you. Stick to your principles, and try not to over-react.

Try to surround yourself with positive people who will pull you up instead of pulling you down. Sometimes this will mean that you actively have to seek the right friends and, unfortunately, learn to spend less time with others. The exception is if you have a definite plan of action in mind to try and 'pull someone up', without allowing the opposite to happen to you. But try to have friends with the same values as you for your children's sake; it will be easier for them to comply with what you expect of them if there is consistency among the adults in their life and they are in contact with other children whose parents expect the same from them.

I have no doubt that a stable and nurturing family is still the best place in which any child, with or without ADHD, can grow up. Give it to your children. Remember that we never own them nor any other person; they are lent to us to look after and to help them to be the best they can be!

A few thoughts about a 'nurturing family'. If there is a father, a mother and children, each one should have his or her place and fulfil their role. The children's role is to grow and develop, bring joy and excitement to the family, and be subjected to parental authority. The mother's role is love and care for the children, and to support her husband. The husband protects his wife and children from 'attacks' and intrusions, gives his wife the love and support she needs and teaches the children to treat her with respect. This is the ideal. Of course, of necessity single parents can and often do manage to provide all these things under difficult and lonely conditions. The most important thing in a child's life is to know that he or she is loved.

You may or may not agree with everything, but why not try it? The amount of discipline needed should be little in comparison with acceptance of the children and the quality time the family spent together.

A final word about relationships. If you ask me what I think is one of the saddest things that can happen in this world? My answer is that when two people who really love one another, tear each other down over money or other less important issues, until nothing but only shredded pieces are left of their love.

Relationships checklist

On the right side award yourself a 1 (not yet the best you can be) or a 2 (your best) and check regularly to see which 1s have become 2s.
Write N/A if not applicable to you.

Be genuinely interested in others.	
Do things together with other people.	
Don't force your views on others.	
Know about 'body language'.	
Do what you say you will do; keep promises.	
Discuss things with people you trust.	
Be honest and consistent with others.	
Admit when you are wrong.	
Look after yourself well (clean and neat).	
Be fair to yourself and to others.	
Deal with anger.	
Do not intrude on another's personal space	

Key strategies

- Communicate, and communicate more!
- Avoid talking behind someone's back
- Given attention and importance
- Spend time with your family ☺

Overcoming Feelings of Failure

If I can really say, "I've been the best me I can be," no guilt should come my way. Don't be afraid to live! Don't give up on life, even if you feel like it. Don't stand back and let life pass you by! None of us can say that we never experience feelings of failure at times. This is a part of life that helps us to grow. The question is: How do you respond to these feelings?

There is a difference between failing to accomplish something and feeling like a failure – in the same way as there is a difference between doing a bad thing on occasion and being a bad person. I know you have heard this before, but you need to view apparent failures as challenges. Learn from them, adjust, and do something in a different way if necessary.

Attempt to get it right from the beginning. How? Make sure your ladder is against the right wall before you climb it! You won't see a sunset if you run east – but if you are convinced that you are running west, go for it! At some stage, you will see the sunset. Don't keep looking back over your shoulder because you will never see it there.

There is an old saying, "Measure twice and cut once" which is very true. Another is, "Water the plants and not the weeds". I accept that it's often difficult not to water both, but in life this means putting emphasis on the good, and not on the bad. If a banana won't peel from the base, try to peel it from the tip. If you struggle with plastic coverings that seem to get stronger as you grow older, always have a small pair of scissors with you!

Look after your belongings and they will 'look after' you. These include your money, your work, your house, your car, your pets, and everything you own. Even your spouse and your children are given to you to care for, though you are not their owner. Look after other people's belongings with as much care and respect – or more – as you do your own.

If you take on new responsibilities or tasks, do them without neglecting the regular ones. For instance, don't get so involved in a particular task that the plants in your garden die because you didn't water them. At least you should make sure that somebody else does it for you when you can't, or invest in a watering system.

There are more than 7 billion people on Earth, but amongst all these people, there is only one person exactly like you. This makes you very special. Only you have your eyes, your ears, hands, feet, brain etc. You may or may not like yourself, but you have to come to terms with it. This is who you are, and what you have, so you might as well use it to the best of your ability.

Tell yourself today, "I am going to be the best me I can be." Not better or worse than others, just the best version of yourself. Then see what a difference this makes in your life. Be grateful for what you have, look after it well and use it for yourself and others. That is all you need to and can do – but be sure to do it. There is a saying, "Use it or lose it". Turning this idea around we can say, "Lose what you don't use", do not let it hold you back. "Use what you have and it will get better" An excellent book to read in this regard is that of Julie Morgenstern, "Shed Your Stuff, Change Your Life"

Apply the BestMe principle to other areas of your life; say to yourself today:
"I will be the happiest me I can be, and I will be the most efficient me I can be."

Say it over and over with excitement, and see what a difference it makes. Come to the point where you say with all your heart, "I only want to be me!" You may include your name as well.

Remember that many important people in history either suffered from ADHD, or had significant features of the condition. Two names that come to mind are Einstein and Winston Churchill. If you study their lives, you will recognise the symptoms. Because of their 'scattered brains' people with ADHD have more 'lateral' thoughts, and may stumble on ideas other people never thought of. If they can only hold onto and pursue these ideas, they can deliver creative solutions and great innovations.

Decisions determine your future, try to make informed decisions, even if you have to ask someone you trust to help you. A decision may be taken on the spur of a moment, but the consequences may last for a long time.

Often, we feel at our most creative when the pressure is on. But you have to train yourself to do things, not only at the last minute, but consistently. This will not come easily by itself, which is why you have to practise the principles outlined in this book.

Having said all this, don't be frustrated if, in spite of all your best efforts, you are still making mistakes. If you suffer from the symptoms of ADHD, you will have an especially hard time doing things consistently right. Don't get discouraged, or feel guilty about it. If you tried your best, this is all you can humanly do. This also applies to your expectations of others.

Say to yourself every day:
"This is the first day of the rest of my life, and I am going to make it my best day."

Learn from the past, but don't dwell on your failures. When you make a mistake, see if there is anything you can learn and do about it – then do it differently next time. Ask yourself, "How long am I going to feel bad about this?" Then answer yourself with, "Maybe 10 minutes, or half an hour!" For this time, **feel really bad!** You may even make a scene of it; then tell yourself, "Stop!" This usually works better than continuing to feel guilty about something you can't do anything about.

There is one thing worse than being poor, and that is not to have a plan. And there is one thing worse than making a mistake, and that is to do nothing. If you do well today, it tomorrow will look after itself and, although you have to plan, worrying won't help you.

Don't, however, be sloppy or irresponsible. The fact that you have symptoms of ADHD should never be used as an excuse to do wrong things or bad things to others.

One thing you have to come to terms with in life is what you can do and what you can't do, even if you do your very best. Only life experience can teach you this. Don't keep on bumping your head against the wall; there will always be a door if you are prepared to look and wait.

Overcoming-feelings-of-failure checklist

On the right side award yourself a 1 (not yet the best you can be) or a 2 (your best) and check regularly to see which 1s have become 2s.
Write N/A if not applicable to you.

Improve the things in your life that bother you.	
Exercise more discipline if needed	
Are you learning from past failures?	
Do you keep up your regular responsibilities when taking on new ones?	
Feel bad about something for a limited time and then stop.	
Listen to criticism, but ignore it if it's untrue.	
How good are you at making the best of situations?	
Are you enthusiastic about life?	
Put more effort into doing what you do best.	
Try to mix with positive people, not joining in with gossip.	
How well are you coming to terms with things you cannot change?	

Final checklist

On the right side award yourself a 1 (not yet the best you can be) or a 2 (your best) and check regularly to see which 1s have become 2s.
Write N/A if not applicable to you.

Budget.	
Healthy eating.	
Exercise program.	
Update your action file if you have one.	
Spend quality time with your children.	
Spend quality time with your partner/friends.	
Stay within the speed limit.	
Provide loving authority for your children.	
Use the BestMe motto and formula.	
A place for everything and everything in its place.	
Walk with something in your hands at home.	
Have a master plan and a master schedule.	
Stick to your promises and decisions.	
Listen well before you speak.	
Take responsibility, don't blame others.	
Get enough sleep.	
Be positive in thought and speech.	
Don't give up too soon.	
Ask for help at the right time.	
Make room for humour in your life.	
Set goals for your life/family.	

A final Word

Some of the thoughts expressed here are my own. Others come from lectures that I've attended and books I've read, not necessarily on the subject of ADHD. I want to mention just a few of my sources that come to mind: Jim Rohn, Jeff Davidson, Anthony Robbins, David Allen, Vic Conant, some information from the book of Christopher Green, and the many speakers I have listened to on the subject of ADHD over the years. This book is a compilation of ideas and I have attempted to put together as many of them as possible. If even one of these ideas helps you, it will make me happy.

I have taken the liberty not to give a detailed bibliography, as this book is not intended to be a scientific dissertation of the subject, only about practical things that work.

"For when the One Great Scorer comes to write against your name, He marks – not that you won or lost – But how you played the game." (Grantland Rice)

There is one more thing that I can think of, that sometimes helped me. When I had to do a boring or uncomfortable thing every day or even more than once a day, I would say to myself "sooner or later there is going to be a last time that I will do this." Looking back quite a few of these activities have had their "last time." Unfortunately, there have also been activities which I enjoyed doing that have had their last time. So, whatever you do, try to make the best of it.

Life is for Living

If you want a reference for any of the information given in this book, contact the Author at bestcanbe@googlemail.com

Editing by Diane Morrison

Illustrations by Dawn Larder

Drawing on page 7 by Rodel

Crocodile drawing by Marius deJager Ebersohn

Appendix 1
What Is ADHD?

ADHD stands for Attention Deficit Hyperactivity Disorder. When children with ADHD are unable to concentrate, but are not hyperactive, some people call it ADD, without the H, but most people just call it ADHD anyway.

> **One in every 20 people has ADHD**

About one in every 20 people has ADHD, so you are always around others who share some of your challenges and are not the odd one out. About one in every 10 people is left-handed, which you probably never notice unless you are right-handed and happen to sit next to a left-handed person at a crowded table. Just so with ADHD – you can probably make it mostly invisible to others.

ADHD was first recognised during the mid-1800s. In 1902, a British paediatrician named George Frederic Still was probably the first to observe and describe it to the Royal College of Physicians. As far back as 1937, it was noted that certain medications might help children who suffer from inattention, hyperactivity and impulsiveness. However, it wasn't until the 1950s and 1960s that medication like Ritalin (methylphenidate) began to be prescribed for ADHD. Today it's prescribed to millions of children and adults.

Most people with ADHD are born with it but, before it's identified, others often think that signs like restlessness and difficulty in concentrating mean that children are naughty or badly brought up. Parents are often blamed for their children's misbehaviour. Boys are more frequently diagnosed than girls when they are young because they tend to be more disruptive in the classroom but, later on, a higher percentage of girls are diagnosed.

> **Many people with ADHD are unusually clever and gifted**

On the positive side, it is also clear that many people with ADHD are unusually clever and gifted, but they need help to channel their activities in the right direction. People with ADHD may be very good at multitasking, solving problems, and handling crises, all of which are good life and career skills. This book will help you control the negative side and bring out the positive side of ADHD.

The basic problem with ADHD centres on low levels of neurotransmitters (substances that help impulses go from one nerve to another) in certain areas of the brain, particularly those that control attention, activity, impulsiveness, and the ability to start and finish tasks. According to the latest research, there are differences in certain areas of the brain, between people (especially children) with ADHD and those not effected. This supports the view that ADHD is basically a neurological condition and not in essence a problem with parenting.

> **Positive thinking and physical exercise can**

There are several of these neurotransmitters, the most important of which are serotonin, dopamine and nor-adrenaline.

Neurotransmitter levels may vary, but the default level for someone with ADHD is low (less than sufficient). However, your levels are naturally increased when involved in physical exercise or when doing something particularly interesting or exciting. For example, children involved in sport often do better with their schoolwork. This is also, why you may be able to sit down for hours and play a computer game or work on a project that really motivates you, but struggle to get through a class or a work meeting that may not grip your attention.

The increase in neurotransmitters will drop again but launching into things with determination and enthusiasm can certainly help you overcome the deficiency. Newer brain research, such as that described by Dr Caroline Leaf in her book: *Who switched off my brain?* describes how the traditional view that our brains are 'hard wired' is not true. The brain's circuits and even its structure can be changed by consistent thought patterns (negative thoughts bring about a decline or shrinking of the nerve cells in our brains, and consistent positive thoughts bring growth and new nerve connections). It could be that some people who have 'outgrown' their ADHD are the ones who have unknowingly applied this principle consistently! Others learn to cope with it, and about one-third really need ongoing medication.

Always remember that ADHD is primarily a medical condition with a physical cause, just like diabetes or a thyroid problem. Don't let anyone convince you that ADHD is mental – that often causes people to give up, go off their medication, or stop doing things in ways that help them cope well with ADHD, making their symptoms worse instead of better. There are environmental factors that may make the symptoms worse, such as problems with relationships or difficulties at home, school or work, but they don't cause it. There are a number of other conditions that also depend on the correct level of neurotransmitters and symptoms of these conditions may overlap with those of ADHD. Some examples are depression and extreme anxiety, which the doctor who diagnoses ADHD has to keep in mind.

The reason why people with ADHD produce low levels of neurotransmitters is still unclear. All we know is that genetic factors may play an important role, so some other members of the family are also likely to have it, or at least the symptoms of it.

ADHD may be present from an early age, but it often becomes more obvious when children attend school, and is most likely to be first noticed by a teacher. Diagnosis is not always easy, and is usually made by a specialist, most often a paediatrician or a psychiatrist who works with children. He or she needs as much information about the person as possible, usually from parents, teachers and the patient. Reports from other professionals may be necessary as well.

Some people are not diagnosed with ADHD until they are adults. This makes it harder for them to adapt because they have built up so many bad habits over the years. If you have not been diagnosed, the best thing to do is to ask your doctor, who may refer you to specialist practitioner who can really help with your particular problem.

Types of ADHD

There are three basic types of ADHD, which show their symptoms in different ways. There are also a number of related conditions, which further complicate the picture and make diagnosis more difficult.

Hyperactive-impulsive ADHD

Some mums notice that their baby is very active even before birth. After birth, ADHD children may be more vigorous and irritable than most babies, and may suffer from stomach cramps. Sometimes they vomit as if they have problems with feeding (this may be true but it's not always easy to tell what is causing it). The child remains very active, always on the go, and may (but not always) walk sooner than most children. They may also have problems with balancing, and take longer to ride a bicycle.

They usually go from one thing to another without finishing anything, and may stay active after bedtime. When they sleep, they may still be restless, often waking up several times during the night. As they grow older, they have lots of energy, as if driven by an engine.

In nursery school and in the classroom, students with ADHD can't sit still and may get up from their chair many times, becoming disruptive. Because of this continual behaviour, they may annoy others and then feel rejected if confronted by other students or their teachers. The problems get worse before they get better, because at first everyone, including their parents, often believes that they are behaving badly on purpose. This can make people with ADHD feel rejected, become very angry inside, start to be rude and continually argue.

People with ADHD don't always understand exactly how they are annoying people. They can't figure out why people respond unkindly towards them, and often feel they are being treated unfairly. They then try to protect themselves by being rude, and they may be excluded for short periods or even expelled from school.

All of this may make it hard to make friends, and easy to become lonely. When you feel lonely, it's tempting to accept friendship from people without thinking much about what kind of people they are. You may find that some of your friends have quite a few problems of their own, whether they have ADHD or not. It is important to have friends who are there when you need them, and to make sure that you are also there for them if they need you. However you should never allow friends to persuade you to do what you know is wrong.

Inattentive ADHD

This is more common in girls, and the problems are initially less obvious. Children may be contented as babies but later become more restless and unable to pay attention for more than a short period. They are inclined to daydream but may also be distracted by what's going on around them. Other children may consider them 'odd' and make fun of them. The symptoms are likely to become more obvious when children start formal education.

Though they may be bright, they often underachieve and may not concentrate well on schoolwork.

With the correct diagnosis and treatment, followed by learning to manage your behaviour, you can overcome the problems associated with this type of ADHD.

Mixed-type ADHD

This is where the symptoms of hyperactivity, impulsivity and inattentiveness are all present at the same time.

Again diagnosis, treatment and understanding can prevent many problems and unhappiness.

Appendix 2
Symptoms of ADHD

These symptoms and signs are documented for interest only and not for diagnostic purposes.

A. Either (1) and/or (2)

1. **Inattention:** Six (or more) of the following symptoms have persisted for at least 6 months to a degree that is inconsistent with developmental level and that impact directly on social and academic/occupational activities. Note: for older adolescents and adults (ages 17 and older), only 4 symptoms are required. The symptoms are not due to oppositional behaviour, defiance, hostility, or a failure to understand tasks or instructions.

    a) Often *fails to give close attention to details* or makes careless mistakes in schoolwork, at work, or during other activities (for example, overlooks or misses details, work is inaccurate).

    b) Often has *difficulty sustaining attention* in tasks or play activities (for example, has difficulty remaining focused during lectures, conversations, or reading lengthy passages).

    c) Often *does not seem to listen* when spoken to directly (mind seems elsewhere, even in the absence of any obvious distraction).

d) Frequently *does not follow through* on instructions (starts tasks but quickly loses focus and is easily sidetracked, fails to finish schoolwork, household chores, or tasks in the workplace).

e) Often has *difficulty organising tasks* and activities. (Has difficulty managing sequential tasks and keeping materials and belongings in order. Work is messy and disorganised. Has poor time management and tends to fail to meet deadlines.)

f) Characteristically avoids, seems to dislike, and is *reluctant to engage in tasks that require sustained mental effort* (such as schoolwork or homework or, for older adolescents and adults, preparing reports, completing forms, or reviewing lengthy papers).

g) Frequently *loses objects* necessary for tasks or activities (e.g., school assignments, pencils, books, tools, wallets, keys, paperwork, eyeglasses, or mobile telephones).

h) Is often *easily distracted* by extraneous stimuli. (For older adolescents and adults this may include unrelated thoughts.).

i) Is often *forgetful* in daily activities, chores, and running errands (for older adolescents and adults, returning calls, paying bills, and keeping appointments).

2. **Hyperactivity and Impulsivity**: Six (or more) of the following symptoms have persisted for at least 6 months to a degree that is inconsistent with developmental level and that impact directly on social and academic/occupational activities. Note: for older adolescents and adults (ages 17

and older), only 4 symptoms are required. The symptoms are not due to oppositional behaviour, defiance, hostility, or a failure to understand tasks or instructions.

a) Often *fidgets* or taps hands or feet or squirms in seat.

b) Is often *restless* during activities when others are seated (may leave his or her place in the classroom, office or other workplace, or in other situations that require remaining seated).

c) Often *runs about* or climbs on furniture and moves excessively in inappropriate situations. In adolescents or adults, this may be limited to feeling restless or confined.

d) Is often *excessively loud* or noisy during play, leisure, or social activities.

e) Is often *'on the go'* acting as if 'driven by a motor.' Is uncomfortable being still for an extended time, as in restaurants, meetings, etc. Seen by others as being restless and difficult to keep up with.

f) Often *talks excessively*.

g) Often *blurts out an answer* before a question has been completed. Older adolescents or adults may complete people's sentences and 'jump the gun' in conversations.

h) Has *difficulty waiting his or her turn* or queueing.

i) Often *interrupts or intrudes* on others (frequently butts into conversations, games, or activities; may start using other people's things without asking or receiving permission, adolescents or adults may intrude into or take over what others are doing).

j) Tends to *act without thinking,* such as starting tasks without adequate preparation or avoiding reading or listening to instructions. May speak out without considering consequences or make important decisions on the spur of the moment, such as impulsively buying items, suddenly quitting a job, or breaking up with a friend.

k) Is often *impatient,* as shown by feeling restless when waiting for others and wanting to move faster than others, wanting people to get to the point, speeding while driving, and cutting into traffic to go faster than others.

l) Is *uncomfortable doing things slowly and systematically* and often rushes through activities or tasks.

m) Finds it *difficult to resist temptations or opportunities,* even if it means taking risks. A child may grab toys off a store shelf or play with dangerous objects; adults may commit to a relationship after only a brief acquaintance, take a job or enter into a business arrangement without doing due diligence.

(From the American Psychiatric Association DSM-5)

Appendix 3
Associated Conditions

In society in general, there are people with a wide range of personalities. These personalities may even be more strikingly different – really unique! – if they contain an element of ADHD.

It is unlikely that there are people with 'pure ADHD.' Because the areas in the brain affected by other conditions like Asperger syndrome, OCD and Tourette syndrome, to name a few, are so closely seated or even overlap *(including 'normal'!)* there is usually some sort of mixed picture present.

A controversial condition, which is also part of the autistic spectrum, is PDA, which stands for Pathological Demand Avoidance; someone trying to avoid everything you ask him or her to do, even the most trivial things, which may lead to an extreme level of anxiety if they are forced to do it.

This has to be distinguished from ODD Oppositional Defiant Disorder, the co-morbid condition most frequently associated with ADHD, which is based more on rebelliousness than anxiety. Anxiety itself is of course prevalent in the general population as well, and so are depression, emotional immaturity and Obsessive-Compulsive Disorder. These co-morbid conditions make the diagnosis and treatment of persons suffering from ADHD much more difficult and, in the adult, should be managed by a psychiatrist knowledgeable about the condition.

Another condition which may sometimes be difficult to distinguish from ADHD is child bipolar disorder. It differs from adult bipolar disorder in that the mood swings are more mixed than typically up and down. Still, elated mood at times and grandiosity are distinguishing features.

If you need further information about the associated conditions, I recommend the excellent book by Martin L Kutscher MD called Kids in the Syndrome Mix...

Useful Resources

These are a few selected organisations that I recommend, based on my personal and professional experiences, where you can get more information about ADHD and other commonly-related problems. The list is very selective and biased toward the UK, but others can be found by searching on the Internet.

Information about ADHD

ADDISS (Attention Deficit Information and Support Service)
www.addiss.co.uk

Marital and Partnership Problems

Specialised advice: www.adhdmarriage.com

Relate: www.relate.org.uk

Even though you may not have any problems with your marriage or relationship just now, you cannot go wrong in enrolling in the internationally acclaimed Marriage Course, which is available at many local venues.

The Marriage Course: www.relationshipcentral.org

Drug and Alcohol Dependency

www.talktofrank.com

I would also recommend that you talk to your GP, as he or she should be able to recommend the best sources of help and support in your area and refer you to experts for help with your underlying problems.

Advice on Debts

The following UK organisations all offer advice with debts and financial problems:

Citizens Advice Bureau: www.citizensadvice.org.uk
(Or visit your local office)

StepChange
www.stepchange.org
08442641919

© Copyright 2017

ISBN: 978-0-244-61720-2
Copyright owner DR MARIUS POTGIETER
Published by: BESTME LTD
bestcanbe@googlemail.com

Copyright Laws and Legal Disclaimer

This document is protected by international copyright law and may not be copied, reproduced, given away, or used to create derivative works without the author's express permission.

This publication is designed to provide accurate and authoritative information with regard to the subject matter covered. It is sold with the understanding that the author and the publisher are not engaged in rendering legal, intellectual property, accounting or other advice. If legal advice or assistance is required, the services of a competent professional should be sought.

Although all of the techniques presented within the pages of this book have been tested and used with very favourable results, it is important to note that everyone with ADHD is unique, and each person will differ on a case-by-case basis.

The guidelines provided are general in nature and can be applied to most people safely. Dr Marius Potgieter can therefore not be held accountable for any poor results you may attain when implementing the techniques or when following any suggestions in the book. Dr Marius Potgieter does not accept any responsibility for any liabilities resulting from the actions of any parties involved.

1. You CANNOT sell or give away the rights to any or all of the information in this book.
2. You CANNOT use the tips to create promotional articles, free reprint articles or e-zine articles.
3. You CANNOT claim copyright to the individual tips unless substantial changes are made that legally separate the original tips with your own re-edited/rewritten tips. You can claim copyright to your own information product(s) as a whole.

This constitutes the entire license agreement. Any disputes or terms not discussed in this agreement are at the sole discretion of Dr Marius Potgieter and the company Bestme Ltd.